AWAKENING
The Healthy Human

Your Best Guide to Becoming
Your Sparkling Vibrant Self

Julie Renee Doering

Awakening the Health Human
Your Best Guide to Becoming Your Sparkling Vibrant Self
Copyright ©2017 by Julie Renee Doering
All rights reserved. Written 2010. Published 2015, 2017.

ISBN-10: 0-9970044-4-4
ISBN-13: 978-0-9970044-4-1

Gable-Kennedy Publications All Rights Reserved.
10 Professional Center Parkway
San Rafael, CA 94903
Info@Julierenee.com

Printed in the U.S.A.

Book design and cover:

No part of this book may be reproduced or transmitted in any form or by any means, electronic or mechanical, including photocopying, recording or by any information storage and retrieval system without written permission of the publisher, except for the inclusion of brief quotations in a review.

Warning – Disclaimer

The purpose of this book is to educate and entertain. The author and/or publisher does not guarantee that anyone following the techniques, suggestions, tips, ideas or strategies will become successful. The author and/or publisher shall have neither liability nor responsibility to anyone with respect to any loss or damage caused, or alleged to be caused, directly by the information in this book.

Endorsement – Disclaimer

Reference herein to any specific commercial products, process, or service by trade name, trademark, manufacturer, or otherwise, in no manner endorses or sponsors the products, processes or offerings.

ALSO BY JULIE RENEE

Books

- Your Divine Human Blueprint
- 100% You Formula
- Quantum Healing Secrets
- Awakening the Healthy Human
- Balance Your Life Now
- Breaking Through
- Illumination

Quantum Academy Certification Training

- Diamond Immersion 7 Day Quantum Ambassador Certification
- Apprentice Trailblazer 12 Month
- Apprentice Essentials 12 Month
- Apprentice Foundational 12 Month
- Immersion Practitioners Training (2–3 year)
- Year of Miracles 12 Month
- Monthly training and events ongoing

Music
- Gratitude: India classical influence harp and vocals
- Pleasures: Celtic harp and vocals
- The Message: Rumi Love Poetry
- Illumination: Harp

App
- Q5 Quantum Meditations in 5 minutes!

All are available online, you may order by visiting http://julierenee.com/programs/

*Dedicated to my dear friends
Charles and Carolyn*

TABLE OF CONTENTS

Preface:
You Are Infinitely More Powerful Than You Know! 1

Out of the Ashes – Phoenix Rising 5

Restoring Your Vibrant Health Authority
and Spiritual Freedom 9

Good Choices Equal Vibrant Health 19

Steps to Break the Pattern of Inaction... 27

Speaking Truth –
Manifesting Health Through Your Vocabulary.......................... 35

Emotional Environment and Great Health................................. 43

Intimate Relationships 47

Vacations 51

Your Spiritual Life.. 55

How to Be Unstoppable in Your Meditation Practice 65

Your Life in Balance 69

Element One – Balance Social and Friends 73

Element Two – Balance Your Emotional Body 77

Element Three – Balance Career.. 81

Element Four – Family and Friends 85

Spiritual Emotional ~ Entanglements 87

Element Five – Finance.. 91

Element Six – Spirituality.. 97

Element Seven – Creativity.. 101

Element Eight – Health and Recreation................................... 105

Clearing Entanglements From the Past.................................... 111

Expelling Obstacles on the Path To Love................................. 115

Completing With Your Parents – Forgiveness 121

Love Gone South - Breakups and Divorce............................... 123

Conclusion 131

Things Our Attorney Wants Us to Share with You................... 133

Precious Advice 137

About the Author... 139

PREFACE: YOU ARE INFINITELY MORE POWERFUL THAN YOU KNOW

You are a radiant being of light. You are divinely connected to the universal source. Your indomitable spirit and astonishing physical body have the ability to generate miracles beyond measure.

You are so powerful. You wield a power beyond your mental awareness. Your commitment and your passionate involvement towards creating and owning your vibrant health are the most important factors in healing.

When you take on the drive of being entirely responsible for your magnificent well-being, your life is truly blessed. This state of existence, when observed with firm resolve, will take you way beyond the standard practice of big business healthcare.

Recovery and Healing – The Journey for Life!

Not a day passes by without someone requesting that I help return their cells to their natural state of wellness and light. I am so grateful for the gifts of healing and wisdom that flow through me, and for the wise elder wisdom that supports my quest to share these unique gifts with my clients and friends so that they may return to health.

Just a tiny bit about my past—in the time prior to when my cells returned to their light state, I experienced: an infant body slightly deficient in all of its structural elements, my first surgery at age three, the ravages of nuclear radiation exposure as a child, multiple forms of cancer for which there was no cure as an adult, a severe pain condition, a violent accident, and 17 surgeries.

I have been gifted with such a challenging life, and I have had numerous close calls with death. I now look upon these experiences as the greatest blessing possible. Without having experienced the depths of breakdown and suffering, I would have never discovered that we are entirely miraculous beings of light. I know with absolute certainty that I suffered all of these horrendous physical maladies to such a great extent so that I could know, without any doubt, the miraculous awareness our bodies possess.

For 17 years, I have dedicated my life to the service of others as a compassionate healer. The courage, love, and strength of so many of my clients have been a driving force for me to reach for more.

How do we move cells from utter darkness and malfunction back into the light of their original God state? This realm of light is where I now dance. Collaboratively, my clients and students join me in the celebration of renewing and restoring life. We are spiritual, scientific researchers and practitioners on the journey back to our miraculous state of existence.

Gandhi, a simple man, a great man, took a stand with calm and absolute resolve to change the world. By the power of his stand, oppression was lifted, and the native people of India returned to governing themselves. Quietly, without fanfare, and without war, he moved a nation, and the world was forever changed.

We all have the power within our bodies to take a stand for our return to lightness and health.

Rectification, Necessary Changes

As the era and the astrological age continue to shift, we are experiencing a natural balancing and correction of imbalances formed during the last 2,000 years of the Piscean (patriarchal) Age. Large, male-dominated organizations are toppling, while an equalization restoration is coming.

Out of a new Age of Aquarius comes the "Age of Androgyny"—the "Age of Equality." Examples are everywhere you look. Even if your personal reference discounts astrology, there is no denying the shift now taking hold.

Think about the visible changes, the changes you are witnessing presently and from the recent past.

Large monetary institutions are radically changing. Out of the recent collapse, there is an increased focus on ones' family values and on creating a slow, steady, financial life. We feel encouraged to enjoy the life we have right now, rather than the old value of decadent excess.

Another patriarchal shift concerns the role of the Old World church. The modern parishioner is now looking for and experiencing, a more personal relationship with the Divine. They look to their priest or pastor as a wise guide. The old (dictatorship) style of running the church that was born out of the demise of the Roman Empire and the rise of the Roman Catholic Church is gently falling away. The spirit seeker is now on a journey of becoming divine. Through prayers, meditation and worship, God is so present to us.

A third apparent shift is the changing face of medicine and the collapse of an outmoded system of healing the sick. So many find no relief from their ills through treatments that are often ineffective and distribute many harmful side effects. Our old medical system will find its place in the new age, but its weight and import will be greatly diminished. A rise in personal responsibility and wellness practices continue to come to the forefront, as we rediscover our divine nature. We were meant to enjoy a vibrant, healthy life. It is time to find the blessing and the wonder of God's perfect plan for each of us.

Let us join in our stand for a healthy lifestyle and take full personal responsibility for our wellness. The practitioners we consciously seek out to assist us in discovering our marvelous state of effervescent health are wise guides; they are light-bearers, illuminating the path to integrated wellness and having a life aligned with our soul's purpose.

OUT OF THE ASHES PHOENIX RISING

"Whenever one door closes, another opens."
—Maria was quoting Reverend Mother in *The Sound of Music.*

Door Closing

Have you noticed your life changing? For example, is the way you are banking and the effective laws governing your banking experience different than your experience of three or four years ago? Are you attending a spiritual organization, church, synagogue or temple? If you still frequent that style of worship, do you see a change towards a more connected, heartfelt association, which is being encouraged for each spiritual aspirant? Does it feel to you like a direct line to the Divine is now becoming available? Have you changed your focus about wellness or your health, or have you started taking a more active role in your wellness? If you have medical coverage, have you noticed a shift towards preventative and wellness programs through your coverage or plan?

In the economic climate of today, we see one institution after another enter into the realm of "crash and burn." There is a profusion of ash and fallout from recent years due to the economic downturn. However, a little-known fact is that ash is incredibly rich in nutrients; these nutrients fertilize the next layer of new emergent growth in the most profound and life-enhancing manner. Similarly, out of the ashes, new versions of these services and organizations are beginning to materialize.

We are experiencing an unraveling of the old, strongly patriarchal systems born out of an era that encompassed the past 2,000 years. From this era, so many good things happened in human history. Many beautiful spiritual teachers surfaced during this period, and through them, we learned about discipline, practice, and patience.

This period was also a time in which we learned about working in organized ways for the benefit of a group or towards the accomplishment of goals. For example, in the recent centuries, we have advanced dramatically in technology and global interaction. Our world has truly become one small planet, as we daily interact, communicate and view our "neighbors" around the world without limitations.

In this time, we also learned from an abundance of poor choices and mistakes we've made. Out of our global, earthly and humanitarian blunders, a core group of individuals what some might name lightworkers, have emerged to lead the way toward more conscious systems, structures and behaviors for all of us to enjoy and participate.

If we were to imagine a visual of the era we are now leaving, a pendulum swinging on its outer reaches would accurately represent the Piscean (male-dominant or patriarchal) Age.

Door Opening

In recorded human history, the era we are now entering into is the first age of balance and equilibrium. Our new realm is the experience of a pendulum in its center position! This is great news for all of us!

As the way we imagine how to be the picture of good health and vitality shifts, we are witnessing our established healthcare institutions changing to stay viable and relevant. The old, established way of business, called medicine, will diminish as a new, well-balanced consciousness surfaces for ordinary, everyday people to enjoy routine health and vitality.

We are disentangling from authoritarian systems. As we do this, we are less inclined to surrender complete control to a dominant individual or organization who wields power over us.

The new sprouts breaking forth in these groups come from the seeds of mutual and collaboratively-efficient and effective institutions. The necessary collapse of the old system ushers in the possibility of an entirely new, fresh approach. The new era, the Age of Aquarius, represents a time of equality, where the playing field is level. Within equality, we also experience androgyny in such a way that both the male and female energies are now active in many people. We are currently well into the Aquarian epoch!

RESTORING YOUR VIBRANT HEALTH AUTHORITY AND SPIRITUAL FREEDOM

I am so grateful for the spiritual training I received in India, as well as here in the United States. A common and consistent theme in my education as a Minister and Master Healer is the practice of spiritual freedom. To observe spiritual freedom means to support all others in their spiritual freedom as well.

The Five Keys to practicing Spiritual Freedom are:

Key one

You are an individual, unique and divine. Your relationship with Source and the flavor of the relationship will be specific to you. All others equally have a unique and sacred relationship with Source and are free to practice this however they choose.

*"There is no way for everyone,
just your way for now until you find another."*
—Rusty Berkus

What a great teaching! Thank God, I discovered this key fairly early on. I have engaged in an exploration of many wonderful religious and spiritual systems. From Christian and Gnostic practices to Native American Ceremonies, to living in India I was privileged to explore the incredible meditations and prayers from the Hindu and Sikh religions and from Sufism.

Here is a story I would like to share with you that I heard while living in India. This story has left a profound and lasting impression on me:

Nine blind men were asked to describe an elephant. Because they could not visually see the elephant, they had to describe it by feel. One by one, the wise men were led to the elephant, and each took their turn describing what they felt.

The first man felt the main body of the elephant. "It's rugged and strong, like a wall," he said.

The next elder took hold of the leg, and after a careful examination revealed his findings. "This creature is like a tree. Feel here, the strong trunk!"

Another reached to the ivory tusk, which he described as a smooth sword. Another declared the ear was much like a banana leaf. On it went until each of them had fully described only that which they could grasp.

Each of the wise men built a strong understanding only involving the part they held. Then they taught their protégées the intricacies of that part.

This is much like what humans have done by describing the Divine, and then creating a path to follow that only involves the piece of God they have known. (Mystics do get to view the whole elephant, and from time to time, we are fortunate to receive a deeper awareness through their teachings.) But without the whole picture, we will always only have a part. There is no lie in that part, but a greater truth is known when all parts are integrated.

A beautiful way to embrace these concepts is to practice tolerance for yourself and toward all others. You don't need others to think the way you think or know what you know. There is room enough for different versions of life and the Divine upon this loving, wonderful planet.

Key two

You have a right to be unique and extraordinary. You have a right to access all the joy and happiness available to you in every moment. All others have a right to be unique and special and to take whatever path they choose.

If we truly practice spiritual freedom, emotional freedom follows. We can, at any moment, lift ourselves up to joy and happiness. We can also choose to follow the rabbit of drama down the rabbit hole. Who you decide to be, and how big you play your game, is up to you. You can choose struggle, from which you may grow and learn as a spirit. However, I want to encourage you to take a stand for your best life, life in which you are passionate and fully self-expressed. Your choice to live life in a large way may require some modifications and improvements on your part. You might observe that the usual responses and behavioral patterns you currently practice may not be valid any longer.

Do you realize the power and passion you wield in your world? Have you thrown yourself in the big frying pan of life and discovered that the richness and loving flavors of your life are getting better and better as you step into being your best, brilliant self?

As Marianne Williamson states: "Our deepest fear is not that we are inadequate. Our deepest fear is that we are powerful beyond measure. It is our light, not our darkness that frightens us most. We ask ourselves, 'Who am I to be brilliant, gorgeous, talented, and famous?' Actually, who are you not to be? You are a child of God. You're playing small does not serve the world. There is nothing enlightened about shrinking so that people won't feel insecure around you. We were born to make manifest the glory of

God that is within us. It's not just in some of us; it's in all of us. And when we let our own light shine, we unconsciously give other people permission to do the same. As we are liberated from our own fear, our presence automatically liberates others."

Take a few moments to reflect upon this quote and upon your current level of joy in your life. Does your inventory of living in your "joy body" conclude that you are an overflowing cup of love, or are you currently living by a choice where you are perhaps blaming and relinquishing responsibility for the circumstances of your life to others? If so, would NOW be a good time to change?

Key three

Must receive permission to heal someone, and they must give themselves permission to heal.

If you are asked to assist someone in their healing, you must ask at each turn if this process is what they are choosing. Through this dialogue, the individual is in control of the shifts they are ready to take on. Leave people alone, who have not specifically asked for your assistance. It is not your right or calling to jump into circumstances you have not been invited to fix.

You may not think that this particular key applies to you if you are not a healing professional. However, I can assure you this key applies to you, as well as to everyone who is living in a human body.

How do we get in the way of others healing themselves? When we start putting our unsolicited information about healing in someone else's space, an avalanche of confusion and unintentional distancing from our loved one's own guidance and inner voice results. It is perfectly fine to ask if your loved one would like your assistance and information. But you need to be able to respect their "yes," "no," or "not right now."

Choosing to be spiritually diplomatic means that you trust and believe in your loved one's ability to access their own information.

Grant them the spaciousness they need to experience the variety of health and wellness options that they are choosing for themselves right here and now.

What is wrong with healing another without their permission? Lacking permission means that you agree to take on the karma and lesson they created for themselves to learn from their situation. If you start healing them and they haven't learned what they wanted to, the problem will resurface at a future point, perhaps in a different version for them to learn.

Would you deliberately want them to revisit that challenge again in their future? We give ourselves all kinds of opportunities to learn and grow. The very fact that humans learn from difficulties means that if you are taking away a learning opportunity (healing without permission), you are robbing your loved one of the chance to take his or her next step as a person. This breach may also prevent them from rising the ladder of energy and vibration, as they may not able to achieve the "wise elder wisdom" they would have gained from their circumstances. If the challenge is taken away, not only is nothing gained, but there is also the possibility that the challenge may come back more intensely in the future.

What if the person is related to you? It does not make it okay to heal without permission, even if you are a blood relative of a person. That person has his or her unique soul path, as do you. When we are talking about small children, that is a different story; you must protect and love them, and shelter them from the storm.

What if a person isn't very smart, and you think you know a lot more about his problem than he does? Do you see how this thought is condescending and doesn't honor the wise spirit of the one in question? He may not be currently accessing his wise self, but under extreme duress, people usually take the leap—whether through prayer or meditation—to listen to that still small voice of innate intelligence.

Key four

It is entirely your responsibility to keep your spiritual, emotional, mental, and physical bodies healthy, happy and clear.

What does it mean to be fully responsible for how life shows up? This is an amazing and eye-opening concept. First, observe any areas of your life where you experience a breakdown of vibrancy. Do you take ownership of the circumstances involving those aspects of your life? Grab a pen and paper and write down all the areas in your life that are not working. Let your mind relax and think about who you have assigned responsibility to in each of these areas.

Now, look at the areas in your life where you feel happy and clear. What are the common denominators that make these parts of your life so stellar? Here are some possible answers:

- You are grounded
- You "work it."
- You do some kind of regular practice
- You have support in place to be successful
- You like the things you are doing
- You identify the happy things in your life as being a great part of yourself
- Happiness is a natural part of your make-up
- You use your mind to fortify yourself when you need a boost
- If you stumble, you have the choice to ask for assistance, but no one owes you your wellness; you create your own wellness by your good choices in every moment.

If you stumble on your path, you have the opportunity to ask for assistance, but no one owes you your wellness. You create vibrancy and joy in all aspects of your life by the good choices you make in every moment.

Imagine taking full responsibility back regarding every challenging situation in your life. Once you have taken responsibility for the scattered pieces of yourself, make a clean, fresh list of these conditions. This time, write down three things that would increase your happiness and ownership in each area. It's time to get actively involved with your fully-embodied, passionate life.

Key five

Whatever energy you put out, more of that kind of energy is given to you.

The more good you put out through your actions or words, the more good will come your way. For example, respect and loving communications are like a beacon for more love and respect to come to you.

This is the essence of spiritual tithing—when you put out good energy, the folks you love, your work, and your environment will all become forces for the goodness that will come back to you.

Likewise, if you focus on what isn't working in your life or if you concentrate on a complaint, you will magnetize problematic energy to yourself. If you are always dwelling on a topic that isn't working, your challenge will compound and get progressively worse. No good comes from dwelling on the negative. A better use of your thoughts and conversations would be to affirm that solutions and vitality are coming to you rapidly.

As we leave behind the past age, we begin to grow a new way of living into our fully-embodied passionate life. A major part of this shift includes the practice of spiritual freedom and personal responsibility.

When we are each personally accountable for our lives, the structures of class and caste fall away. We are moving into an age where a person's true worth is measured by their ability to be a valuable member of society, a contributor.

Think about a time when you performed an act of selfless service. Remember showing up for work, and without question, working alongside whoever had come that day?

As a Realtor with Seville Properties, one of the most prestigious real estate brokerage firms in California, I remember taking a weekend to participate in a "Christmas in April" project for a needy family in East Palo Alto, California.

A strong black woman headed the family we served. She had the countenance of a lady who had seen many hard times and who had formed a resolve to endure. She was single and had likely raised her children alone. Now she was continuing the journey by raising four of her grandchildren.

There must have been forty of us working to give her tattered, rundown home a total refresh and renewal. Among the people volunteering were young and old, workers and business people. No one was better than another. We were a team working to accomplish a common goal. The house and its new plumbing system were miraculously completed within our allotted time. I was so deeply touched by the look of appreciation on the grandmother's face; the softness and surrender were overwhelming.

During this project, who we were did not matter. What we owned did not matter. How skilled we were with tools did not matter. We were all a valuable part of the team.

This team of equals is so much the metaphor for the age we are now entering. We will have new ways of interacting and new common threads that weave us together in peace and love.

The ashes of the Piscean Age and the collapsing patriarchal structures open us to a more self-ignited collaborative society. We grow from all the wisdom we have accumulated over the centuries, and we find the door wide open for co-creation. We are in the foundational period of the new era. Setting the groundwork for a new way of being and a new path for discovering yourself as a

"Healthy American" begins today. What we choose now and how we direct our energies and actions will lay the groundwork for the next 2000 years.

Contemplations

When you hear the words, "healthy" and "human" together, what comes to mind?

If this image was less than positive, what could you imagine to help brighten the concept of being a Healthy Human?

Can you imagine yourself and your "tribe" engaging in a co-creative lifestyle?

GOOD CHOICES EQUAL VIBRANT HEALTH

The lifestyle you choose to live, and the importance you put on the integration of your spirit with your physical connection, will prove poignant in your overall health and longevity. If you are currently experiencing an interruption in a flow of vibrant health, this is a great opportunity for you to slow down and notice what choices you made along the way that may have led to the state of health you now know. You may also then see some intuitive feelings or thoughts emerging as to the kind of behaviors you could begin to practice to restore yourself to full vitality.

When I reflect on how my saga of illness began, I remember the circumstances that were occurring the year before my diagnosis of terminal cancer. I was in an impossible marriage. I was unhappy beyond belief with the relationship. I was in a deep depression with no communication skills to manage the onslaught of poor behavioral choices and words coming from my mid-western farmer husband.

He was a country boy, lacking in sophistication. He was young, round, and he loved his brew. Meanwhile, I was a thin, fragile bundle of layers. Together, we were a confusing relationship fabric tied together with a piece of twine.

My dark hair draped down to my waist. I always had a baby on one hip, and often, the other hanging off my shoulders or in a front pack. I found my only joy in raising our two, radiantly beautiful, blonde-haired, blue-eyed, little girls.

I was so unhappy in my marriage that I wanted to leave. But we were so poor; it appeared that there was no escape. I grew more depressed by the day. My friends from church stopped coming around. They told me it hurt them too much to see my husband being rude to me and treating me unkindly.

Early in the pregnancy of my third child, I fell ill. I became too weak to stay awake and care for the girls. My house, which had always been a bit on the wild side, became an absolute disaster zone. By the fourteenth week, I heard what no one wants ever to hear: I was so ill, they could not assure me that I would survive through the ensuing surgeries and treatments they said I needed.

I took to praying three hours a day. I endured two surgeries while pregnant. I would not abort. So after they spoke of it once, they never returned to the subject.

I, of course, did survive against all odds and gave birth to a healthy boy. He weighed in at 8 pounds at birth, while I, at 5'6", weighed in at 104.

Our marriage was clearly over, and after the birth and a prolonged hospital stay, I moved out on my own.

Everyone has a story of illness and the circumstances that developed before their cells losing their sparkle. This story may be much like your own story, or maybe you have a very different story. Or perhaps you have been blessed with wonderful health, yet you witness those you love enduring difficult circumstances.

Either way, there are some essential elements to notice about the events leading up to how it is that we become ill. There are also things that lead us to create our good health.

Mental Body Breakdowns
- Harmful stress
- Inaction
- Unwillingness or inability to see positive choices
- Financial stress
- Not speaking the truth
- Complaints or continuing to engage in victim behavior
- Using the kind of vocabulary that does not support the manifestation of health

Emotional Environment Influences
- The state of your intimate relationships
- Friends
- Vacations
- Future plans

Spiritual Influences
- Connection with the Divine
- Prayer and meditation practice
- A community who shares your values and principles
- Your chakras
- Golden rings what most people call a halo
- Spiritual body connection
- State of your aura

Physical Influences

- Good nutrition—nurturing your mental, emotional, spiritual, and physical bodies
- Relationship with your physical body
- Physical activity
- DNA and hereditary factors

Let's examine these influencers more carefully…

Mental Body

"What the mind can imagine and hold onto as true it will manifest in physical reality."

Harmful Stress

What are your consistent thoughts? Are they useful? Do they help you enjoy your day? Do you enjoy the flow? Are your thoughts in the happiness vibe?

One reason the human body breaks down is that the worrisome thoughts we think are not high enough energetically to produce ongoing good health. When I was depressed, my recurring thoughts were resonating at low energy frequencies.

In my vibrant health, I am often in a state of blissful calm. My recurring thoughts move in the direction of appreciation, gratitude, and contribution. I am often pondering action steps for my next project and celebrating the breakthroughs produced in my practice.

Let's take a look at what is happening for you at this moment. Take out a pen and paper and answer the following questions:

- What factors in your life may fit in the harmful stress category?
- Is there a way you could move the toxic stress down a few notches and eventually move it out of your life altogether?

Whatever we focus on becomes our reality, so if you want to be a force for change in your life, or in the world, concentrate on the change you want to be.

Think about your frequent complaints. How often during the day do you revisit those things you are not happy? Ten times? 100 times? What are you telling yourself over and over again? If you are looping around in a consistent complaint, you are not in the space of creating a miracle from the inside out.

The internal environment of a miracle is the environment of endless possibility. It is powered by the firm belief that you have a right to live vibrantly in abundance and excellent health.

Secret Shifters to Get Into Your Joy Body

- Let go of the past. Forgive yourself and all others for whatever didn't work out. Replace whatever didn't work out by remembering how loved you are. Include some happy thoughts about how things always work for your good.
- Get happy with who you are. Let go of your self-editing and critical inner conversations. You are awesome. Feel what it feels like to love yourself. Cool, huh? Stay in the state of loving yourself. Don't worry; you're not going to become a narcissist. When you love yourself, you love all others, too. Your affinity for nature and life expands tremendously.
- Negativity and low energy are contagious; they're like a social virus. If you caught some of these while you were going about your beautiful day, as quickly as you can, do a happy activity and release the negativity. Don't spend a moment blaming someone else for giving you the negative energy. It is entirely your job to keep yourself uplifted and joyous.

When I catch a negative energy virus, I:
- Chant exquisitely divine mantras in my garden
- Go to a romantic comedy and get some laughter rolling
- Listen to my favorite inspirational speaker (at the moment, Jack Canfield)
- Light a scented candle and take a bubble bath
- Curl up on the sofa and read a great book
- Play my favorite compositions on my marvelous harp
- Take out the watercolors and create a superb piece of art
- Create a stunning necklace (string pearls and stones)
- Run around a pristine lake on top of Mount Tamalpais

Take out a pen and paper and create your "Shifter List." When you are shifting a behavioral pattern, you will want to make a few copies of this list; hang one on your bathroom mirror and the other in your kitchen.

Remember, you are in charge of your feelings and your state of mind. What would you do if you stayed in this state ongoing? Who would you be? What is your dream life?

"The state that you are in, at any given moment, determines your perception of reality, and thus, your decisions and behaviors. Your behavior is not a result of your ability, but rather the state that you are in, in this moment."
—Anthony Robbins

Let's take this concept a bit further. How do you discipline the mind to stay forward moving and positive, regardless of how your outer circumstances are flowing at the moment?

Are you diving down a rabbit hole, or are you reaching toward the heavens?

There was a point in my life when I decided to call an end to the drama. My life was full of tough circumstances, which included a long-term cancer treatment, a severe pain condition, a brutal accident that left me wheelchair bound, and an unlucky stream of relationships that never seemed to go the distance or provide me with the haven I longed for. I distinctly remember the very day everything started to turn around. It had occurred to me that, even if difficult things were happening, I would choose to find a space of gratitude for the opportunities that were before me; I would hold each experience as a lesson that would help me to grow.

When I made this decision, I am sure I was one of the biggest "rabbit hole runners" of the entire century. I seemed to dive down a rabbit hole every chance I got. Let me explain what that means...

"Rabbit Hole Diving Behaviors"

- Having long conversations with everyone who will listen about how difficult life is
- Finding other friends to commiserate and listen to everything that is wrong in their lives
- Amplifying a problem, churning on it and broadcasting it
- Being in the state of "poor me, I am innocent" and "they are at fault."
- Attracting more drama partners who were committed to experiencing life difficultly

Making the choice to find the wonder and opportunity in my life was a huge step!

Promises for Shifting Out of Drama

- Focus on the goodness and rightness of everything
- Stop blaming and take responsibility
- Stop rehashing the past
- Quickly end conversations that bring you down the rabbit hole
- Adopt an attitude of gratitude

When you get off the drama cycle, you take a step in the direction of being a powerful contributor in the world. With your new found power—funded by a mind aligned with a loving Universe that is working for your good and the good of all others—you can move rapidly into a state of unconditional love. What you do with this state of being has no limits.

When the mind focuses on blessings, we can move towards great accomplishment and the creation of daily miracles. What could you do if you stopped going down your rabbit hole?

Along with quieting the mind and committing to ending the drama in our lives, let's explore some of the other traps from the mind that detach us from joyful, life-giving energy.

Inaction

Another malady of the mental body is inaction. Imagine a time when you felt stagnant or stuck, where you were unable to take your next step or move in a forward direction. Can you recall an occasion or two where you found yourself stuck and unable to shift out of a negative situation, even though you knew in your heart of hearts it would have been so much better for you to have done so? By staying stuck, your mind started playing tricks on you. Perhaps you started imagining things and got a little paranoid. Inaction is a real brain freeze.

STEPS TO BREAK THE PATTERN OF INACTION

- Perform rigorous exercise. One of my favorite breakthrough-into-action techniques is to go for a brisk run. You can do a 90-day exercise program, train for a triathlon, or take up mountain biking. Activity, especially outdoor activity, helps break through the crippling wall of inaction.
- Do a guided meditation. By practicing my Definitive Guide to Meditation, found at JulieRenee.com, you will clear all energy channels and give yourself a spiritual shower from the inside out. Often moving everyone else's energy out of your body gives you back your confidence, your certainty, and your ability to move forward
- Check in with yourself and your emotional body. Are you in fear? To accomplish the outcome you wish to achieve, have you made room in your psyche for good results? Do you have a structure for moving forward that is understandable and fits you? If these are issues, create a plan of action to improve your situation 5% a week until you are where you want to be.

- Clear family patterns out of your cells. Your body is a blueprint of your parents' encoding. All of the body wisdom gleaned from generations previous to their birth are accumulated to form your body and the temperament you exhibit. You are a melting pot of half you mother and half your father. There are also a couple of chromosomes that are uniquely you. A common thought is that DNA gives you your body type and structure, and that is, indeed, true. Also found in the DNA are the survival patterns from your family line. That means that if your DNA is programmed with ancient slave or indentured servitude pictures, this DNA programming will affect your cells, which could negatively impact your ability to move forward. Removing these patterns (such as through the DNA clearing work I do) is helpful if you have already tried the "Inaction Resolvers" and have made little progress.
- Stop being unwilling or unable to see the positive choices that are put before you. Sometimes a person just gets in the zone of ignoring his own inner guidance system. After a while, the helpful advice from friends gets erased, and the self-created blinders become a real handicap. Are you listening to your guidance systems? If you can only see negative choices on your path, I can guarantee you've missed the positive downloads from your higher self that are there for you and that are free for the taking.

You and only you can turn this behavior around. Until it shifts, you will live life in a constant flow of negativity. Find some good audio listening programs and videos on the power of positive thinking. These will help you start shifting your negative patterns of thinking. Speakers I enjoy listening to while I am driving include Jack Canfield, Tony Robbins, and Joel Osteen. I also like listening to my own CDs, as they uplift and inspire me. There are many good inspirational speakers and coaches. Find the ones that lift you up and rotate their programs until you are back in the positive flow of possibility.

Financial Stress

Have you had a time in your life where your finances weighed heavily on you? Perhaps through a series of unforeseen circumstances, you lost your job or your ability to work for a while and things unraveled for you financially. What are the repercussions of financial stress?

I have historically been a worker bee. When my health is good, I am working to produce money and support my happy life. I was a little entrepreneur; I began earning money as a five-year-old. I would sit by the crib of a neighbor's baby and quietly play, while our mommies had a cup of coffee and shared neighborhood gossip. I would bring in a nickel each time I did that. As I grew, I babysat, sewed velvet bow ties for the boys in choir, ran a childcare summer program, sold Avon door-to-door, and worked as a hostess at the new Burger King down the block.

Being a little go-getter, I had the ability to earn money easily. What I didn't understand was how to manage my money, how to budget, and how to create a safety net for myself as an adult.

As a young divorcee, for the first time in my life, I found myself armed with a bunch of department store credit cards. While married, my husband and I had absolutely no disposable income. We ran a family farm during the collapse of family farming across the Midwest. I had no new personal items for many years. When I received my first credit cards, the process of spending with plastic was entirely new to me. I found it exhilarating to purchase new clothing and household items on a whim. Unfortunately, I rapidly accrued significant debt, in comparison with the modest income I earned while attending college. I had to take a few steps back and look at what I was doing.

The numerous and frequent phone calls from creditors asking for immediate payment was frightening. My mental environment was now one of severe, unrelenting stress. Daily internal pressures pounded away at my nervous system, putting me on high alert. Instead of sinking into the wonderful state of receptive healing and regeneration sprung from a relaxed nervous system, my body was breaking itself down. I lived in a level of stress that was not conducive to the healing my body longed for.

I considered filing bankruptcy since I was desperate to get out from under the weight of debts. What I didn't understand back then was that all aspects of one's life need to be in balance. To accomplish balance, I needed to consciously plan my "energy expenses," which included financial management.

I chose not to file bankruptcy and began working three jobs while being a full-time student. My goal was to get caught up with my credit card payments over the next few years. I had a grueling schedule that allowed me only three hours of sleep each night. I was in school at 8 AM, followed by house-cleaning jobs, work at a police department as a graphic artist, and then I'd go to my full time, night job as a waitress. I would get home between 11 PM and 1 AM, at which time I would study for my next day's classes. A big pot of caffeinated black tea helped me to stay awake every night. I somehow managed to keep my grades high and excelled in my work environments. I was even promoted to head the department at the Crime Prevention Center, along with being the top paid waitress in the fine dining restaurant where I worked.

Still, the toll on my body from this exhausting schedule kept me in a state of physical challenge, and my medical tests continued to reveal recurring poor results.

What is your current level of ease or stress concerning your financial life?

Are you noticing a curtailing of happy activities or a reduction of light-hearted laughter as you go about your day?

Is it time to take stock of your financial situation and upgrade your relationship with your financial life?

Turning It All Around – Awake and Aware

My number one recommendation for anyone who has not yet brought their financial life into sparkling pristine order is to find a good system to effect change. You may not yet have the information you need, but with a little assistance from the masters of money management, a few weeks from now things will be so much smoother.

Resources for Straightening Up Your Personal Finances

Books

Suze Orman's books are reliable, trustworthy guides to better living through conscious management of your financial life.

When I was stepping it up, I began to affirm: "I am a master of finance!"

A few years ago, I used Suze Orman's book, *Courage to be Rich,* did all the chapter assignments, and now have a stellar financial picture. That was an excellent eye opener for me. As I went through each chapter, and cleaned up and discovered how to create my joyful financial security, my stress levels dropped dramatically. As my money life came into balance, my mind found deep abiding peace.

Suze also provides the forms for a Will and Trust, Durable Power of Attorney, and Health Care Directives—all available in a download. Her system totally rocks! I loved using it because, for every place that required a response, I could push a button and have Suze's attorney's voice come on and exactly explain what I needed to consider before answering each question and filling in the blanks.

There are many excellent books out there. Do the book option if you are a self-starter, and follow the directions well.

Financial Counselor

This is an excellent option if you need some hand-holding and prefer the validation and support of another person.

Things to consider when selecting a financial counselor:

What are the main areas to address that can bring grace and ease to your financial life?

1. Income and a means to support your life and lifestyle
2. A savings account

    a. The first savings account is for planned spending, including the things that you know will come up that are not included in a monthly budget

    b. The second account is a rainy day fund, which consists of six months of expense funds to cover you if you should decide to take a break from generating income or have an emergency situation that prevents you from working

3. A retirement fund/plan in place
4. Insurance, including home or renters insurance, car and health insurance, and life insurance
5. Investments and your home
6. A current net worth statement
7. A manageable spending plan or budget
8. A debt repayment plan (if you are experiencing debt)

With these financial keys in place, you will be on the road to your happy life.

Another process that comes from the mental body is our powerful use of language.

SPEAKING THE TRUTH— MANIFESTING HEALTH THROUGH YOUR VOCABULARY

"The words you habitually choose affect how you communicate with yourself and therefore what you experience."
—Anthony Robbins

In this section, we will explore two crucial elements of the healthy mind/healthy body connection. The first concept involves the amplification of personal power and fulfillment through the practice of speaking truthfully. The second concept reveals the effect of our vocabulary on all aspects of our health and happiness. Your mental, emotional, spiritual and physical health will take great leaps of progress as you integrate these vital truths into your habitual way of being.

Personal Power and Fulfillment—Speaking Truthfully

Do you want to increase your manifesting power by 100%?

How is your truth-telling barometer these days? Are you always impeccable with your word? Below is a lesson to help you amplify the power of your words to increase your manifesting power. Just do your best and don't stress. Over time, as you practice these concepts you will get better and better at them.

Take a piece of paper and a pen, or your laptop, and answer the following questions honestly:

1. When I relay information, do I embellish the truth to suit my needs?
2. If you answered yes, ask yourself: When I embellish the truth does some part of the communication become untrue?
3. When late or put on the spot, do I make excuses that are unrelated to the circumstances?
4. Do I have the belief that sometimes telling the truth is cruel?
5. If you answered yes, ask yourself: Can I shift how I perceive truth-telling? Can I think of truth-telling as a form of loving, respectful communication—the kind of conversation that would be beneficial to all parties involved?
6. When I speak about the truth, is it truly the only truth? For example, is it a reality based entirely on my perception of what I think others should believe, or can I enjoy a diversity of viewpoints?
7. Have I lied to myself while answering any of these questions? (Remember, do your best and don't stress. The goal is to bring consciousness into your relationship with truth so as to increase your manifesting power.)

Think about a time when someone told you something that you knew, or suspected, was untrue. Can you feel the feeling of being lied to? Notice what are you feeling and where in the body you are feeling it.

Perhaps you felt odd, dull, angry, offended, betrayed, or disrespected. All of these feelings, and any others you are noticing, are in the lower frequency of vibrations. Think about this: something somebody shared with you just lowered your spiritual wattage—

possibly dramatically. Imagine walking around all day reducing your wattage a bit here and a bit there. Each time you tell an untruth you lower your wattage. Will the universe believe you when you claim your outrageous abundance? Will you be bright enough to match the energy of your abundance picture?

Going a little deeper into this concept, let us think about each of us humans as beings of light.

In the DVD, *Messages from Water*, Dr. Masaru Emoto, a Japanese researcher, froze water molecules and observed them under a microscope to study the effects that words and music had on the molecules. He discovered that positive words like love and happiness made beautiful, lacy, ice crystals. Negative words made ugly spider webs and dismal manifestations.

When you contemplate the fact that our human body is over 90% water, you can get a good idea as to why we respond so strongly to loving or harmful communications, because, either way, our cells change.

Our natural state is one of light and love. So, when speaking truth, we easily move into the state of light—the state of creation or perfection. Further, Neuroscience has discovered that our brains are wired to be social or to respond to other brains and that healthy relationships have a beneficial impact on our health, as explained in the book, *Social Intelligence*, by Daniel Goleman. As the book progresses, he states that we can "catch" an emotion, just like a virus, so if someone "emotes on you," your brain, and then the cells of your body, will come down to that negative state. On the other hand, if someone smiles at you, your brain and body lighten and respond to that higher emotion. I mention this to bring home the point that we are deeply responsive beings, and we all have the ability to go to the lightest vibration. If someone shares their negativity with you, you can "reboot yourself" by focusing on a positive feeling, or something beautiful in nature

In David Hawkins' book, *Power Versus Force*, he uses kinesiology, which is basic muscle testing, to test the vibration of many things regarding their relationship with pure truth. In his findings, he discovered that Hinduism had the highest vibration of any of the larger religious practices on Planet Earth. I have a few theories as to why this is so:

1. The religion, in some form, has been practiced for thousands of years.
2. The prayers are spoken in Sanskrit, which is the language of truth, meaning that the sounds/words are the vibrations of the thing or concept being spoken about. Very cool!

   While in India, I had the privilege of studying with Brahmin priests in the Vishwa Shanti Ashram. Their scriptural texts were the Vedas and the Yogic Sutras, along with other divine texts. The Vedas are considered the highest truth. There are four Vedas. Each of these treatises is complete in themselves and represent a different branch of study of the truth. Three of the Vedas are visible and available for study. The fourth Veda is a sacred book of incantations that remains hidden to the world. This book contains the words and sounds that control the physical world. As such, they are left in the hands of the holiest individuals.

If you are interested in a Hindu text of pure truth that is accessible and of truly the highest vibration, I suggest you read the Yogic Sutras of Patanjali. These thoughts, which are truly poetic, have stimulated in me many euphoric and blissful moments.

Thinking back again to the concept of language as truth, Sanskrit is a perfect example of that which is 98% accurate. We can compare the English language in its basic spoken form and surprisingly discover it is in the 10% range of truth. The fact that the English language is more a descriptive device than a language of truth means that our words don't line up as the vibration of the concept or thing we are talking about. This may encourage an overall cultural theme of speaking untruths within our social structure.

However, you can, with clear intention use the English language to speak truthfully. It takes clear intention and attention to all the little details.

(Remember what I said earlier: do your best, don't stress.) Drop your perfect pictures. This is a process of raising awareness and consciousness. It is not a process meant to be done overnight, but rather a profound lifelong learning. Your best effort at any given time is enough.

The ultimate goal of this lesson is to increase the power of your word in the universe. When you increase your truth ratio, you increase your power, resulting in your ability to use your words as a powerful tool to create your wondrous reality.

Health and Happiness through Uplifting Vocabulary

What the mind believes creates your reality. How your brain interprets, your world comes from your consistent use of language. Who you are and how deeply you live your passionate life is directly related to the things you tell yourself and others over and over again. Also, how big you play and the level of which you deeply enjoy your word is expressly related to your choice of syntax. Let me give you an example:

I have had a habit of being delighted with my work, but of also feeling spent by the end of my day. When my close friends ask me how I am, I tell them that I am happy and tired. In fact, my end of the day mantra has consistently been: "I am so tired." I discovered this flaw in my speaking just last week and enthusiastically have put into place a new end of day mantra—"I am relaxed and blissful."

By slightly altering those words, my mind now believes everything is in perfect order, and my body is following suit. When I said, "I am tired," my body complied and gave me exhausted, worn out feelings. However, by saying, "I am blissfully relaxed," as my new mantra, I have been experiencing many more enjoyable evenings. One night, I found I had so much physical energy I could go and do a Turbo Jam aerobic workout. It was super fun!

Here are some examples of words you could be using to hypnotize yourself with negatively, and some empowering alternatives you can try out to replace the low energy expressions.

Angry	Mildly Disenchanted
Anxious	Excited
Down	Mellow
Embarrassed	Vibrantly Aware
Frightened	Challenged
Hurt	Surprised
Irritated	Stimulated
Jealous	Admiring
Lonely	Self-actualizing Time
Nervous	Attentive
Overwhelmed	Abundant Opportunities
Sad	Sorting Through My Thoughts
Sick	Cleansing
Stressed	Blessed

Think about the words you use on a daily basis to describe your state of being. Imagine yourself going through your day, walking, going to the mirror, sharing a meal, working, relaxing later in the day, your home time and your bed time. Where are you listening to yourself and hearing words that consistently lower your energy?

Take a moment to write down those words or phrases that bring you down. Then write down a couple of uplifting or diffusing words or sayings to replace them.

Do you notice any key phrases that lower your vibration? Experiment this week by altering those key phrases. See what happens when you lighten the energy-lowering verbiage by replacing them with strengthening expressions.

Using words to alter your mental and emotional state can be surprising and invigorating!

EMOTIONAL ENVIRONMENT AND GREAT HEALTH

Your emotional environment is a major key to having excellent physical health. How you feel about yourself at any given moment can make a world of difference as to how you progress through life, health and having a vibrant career.

Do you love yourself? This can be quite a stretch for some folks. Maybe you are even asking yourself what that means. Perhaps you are not sure if you love yourself or not. Review the following statements and see where you align in this experience of loving yourself.

1. I love myself exactly the way I am. At any given moment, I can try on new habits and behaviors. But for today, I am thrilled with the version of me I am currently expressing.

   Questions:
   • What words trigger a "yes"?

   • What words trigger a "no"?

   • Is there something you are holding yourself back from expressing?

- Do you have an idea of needing to be perfect to meet someone else's standard? If so, could you let go of perfection and move to blissful celebration?

2. I take wonderful care of my body, the temple of my spirit. I make good choices regarding my healthy lifestyle, choosing foods that are right for me and vibrant activity to keep my body finely tuned and joyous.
Questions:
- Are the activities and actions related to your physical body adding to your vibrant longevity?

- Do you enjoy your body; is it fun to be in?

- Can you depend on it to operate well for the daily tasks you set out to accomplish?

3. I feel so connected and blissfully part of life! I have friends and family members who get me, and I get them!
Questions:
- Are you part of everything or have you taken yourself out of the game?

- When you do connect with others, do you experience a magnificent connection most of the time?

4. I am the master of my universe. My will is powerful, and I can live in sync with my vision for myself!
Questions:
- Are my desires lined up for success?

- Do I have many conflicting desires that leave me feeling ineffectual?

5. My love awaits me everywhere I go. As I source love and share it, love is always the energy waiting for me in all circumstances.

Questions:

• Have I found the practice of gratitude fueling my love vibe?

• Do I trust that everything I bring into my life has a purpose and is in divine order?

• Am I a beacon of love?

That was fun! Now let's move into a conversation about intimate relationships. Having friends and family who you love and share love with is vital to your healthy functioning organic system. Our brains have a whole area devoted to emotional and social behaviors. When we are loving and feel loved, we do much better than when we are feeling isolated and alone.

INTIMATE RELATIONSHIPS

To be emotionally healthy you must enjoy strong relationships with friends and family members. The quality, ease, and joy of those companionships are as important as the existence of them.

I have been working with a middle-aged woman, who is recovering from a profound illness where she almost lost her life. She was a woman of the church who left the convent, eventually married, and who now has a handsome preteen son. Her relationship with her life partner had been strained for some years when she became sick with illness. Although love was sometimes present between them, they also engaged in a lot of conflict and disharmony.

The conflicts began when her husband's real estate business started to falter due to the economy. He was a real estate tycoon, but now he was facing multifaceted problems within a toppling industry.

Many of this former nun's symptoms stemmed from the breakdown of her digestive system. Her life had become difficult to digest—literally. Part of her healing journey has been to calm and soothe her mind and to bring a gentle, loving vibration into their relationship.

We are so lucky to have the amazing regenerative components of the physical body at our beck and call. At any moment, we can change our minds, get into the happy, grateful flow of life, and return to our healing, restorative space.

Love is the greatest healer of all.

Last week, after a wonderfully busy action packed week, my dear friend, Chris, blessed me with a personal visit! This is a big deal because his commute from Berlin, Germany to Marin County, California is a bit of a hike. Chris and I have been the dearest of friends for a good ten years. However, our meetings are few and far between. He walked into my home, sunshiny, his heart alight with a hop, skip and a jump in recognition of our "soul family" meeting. After a quick catch up conversation, we sat on the sofa, holding each other for a leisurely hour. Refreshed and remembered, he continued on his way, both of us lighter and brighter for the brief and joyous reunion.

Relationships can add to your joyous health or detract from it. If your relationship rocks—like my friends, Larry and Pam at Unity Church in Novato, CA—you live in a vacuum of love, good feelings, and happiness. This would make you one of the lucky ones who will experience the healthy benefits of love in balance.

If, however, you are struggling with a different picture, for example, if you are living in a relationship fraught with difficulties, perhaps you need to rethink the relationship.

At any moment you have the power to raise the vibration for yourself. If your partner wants a more joyful, happy experience, then seek out a good love life coach. Definitely, take the time to make an effort. Bringing your love life into good health is so necessary for longevity and physical vibrancy. You know what to do if your companion wants to stay angry or unhappy—shift to a space where you and your beautiful body can be in a safe, loving, neutral zone, and then move into a place of extreme gratitude!

If you are alone, hey, that's not so bad! You can allow yourself to relax into the experience of being single while remaining deeply connected to all others. Relish the wonderful hugs and hands that you joyfully come in contact with throughout your day. There is always a plethora of children who need a good squeeze and a cuddle. Babysit for your friends and celebrate the amazing love you have all around you. There is so much to be grateful for.

Because I am not partnered with a significant other presently, my father said, "Well Julie, I guess you are my old maid daughter." Believe me; I am far from that image of the old maid. I think of an old maid as a spinster who lives in the library or who crochets doggy doll toilet roll covers for fun. There is nothing wrong with those activities; they are great if you are a senior and enjoy creating. But what I am saying about myself, and all others who find themselves without a life partner at the moment is that we are not defined by a partnership or a lack of one; **we are defined by our love and contribution to all others.** If you are connected and living your life fully self-expressed and in balance, then you, my dears, are right on track!

VACATIONS

When was the last time you went on your best-ever vacation? Has it been awhile? Are there places you would like to go that are on your someday list? What would you have to do to get yourself started?

My all-time favorite vacation was the time when I spent a half year in India. A close second was a trip I took through several countries in Europe, where I followed the trail of the King Author legends.

I went to India at age 33, feeling pulled to go. I sold my house, put my possessions in storage, and with very little preplanning, got on a plane heading in the direction of India! I landed in Bombay, rested for 12 hours, then proceeded to shop for saris. The odd thing was that I went out and bought five regal-looking saris, and with little help, was wrapping those saris correctly and wore them from the first day I arrived. My four bags of clothing became a bit of a nuisance, and I donated many of them during my ashram stay at the Ganeshpui Ashram where I visited the spiritual adept, Gurumayi during my first four weeks in India.

My meditations had become sweeter and deeper the year before the journey, so the experience of being in an ashram dedicated to spiritual growth and awakening using meditation and chanting was a blissful dream come true. Our early morning chanting was called "Seva," (selfless service). Then we had "Darshan," (sitting with the guru), followed by more evening chanting. This made every day feel otherworldly. The routines of western living fell by the wayside as the rhythms of chants and meditations rose to the surface of my waking moments; it was utterly enchanting. My every breath and quieting mind eventually became a meditation and a prayer. I began not to delineate the difference between meditation and sleep; it all felt the same to me—profound, peaceful and life enhancing.

I left the Ashram to connect up with my dear friend, Hannah Shirah's Guru, who was leading a peace pilgrimage through India. Hannah had to cancel her trip at the last minute and asked if I would take her place as Ambassador of Peace from Minnesota. Since I was already planning to be in India, this opportunity suited me well. I traveled from Bombay to Bangalore and experienced my first night at a luxury hotel in Bangalore at the Holiday Inn. It was a real luxury: marble throughout, countless people to serve you and beauty—so much lusciousness!

India was a real coming home for me. So many incredible memories lay in a rich environment of emotional pleasures. While in India I was seen as the spiritual master I am. I experienced being loved and treasured and welcomed with such intensity. Everywhere I traveled, there were eyes of love and acceptance awaiting me.

I have always said my months in India were the most important life passage I have ever experienced. It is one thing to give birth to children, which is an absolute miracle! And it is an entirely different thing to give yourself the gift of an enormous soul journey.

Do you understand the importance of giving yourself time for fueling your emotional body and your memory tank with the exotic, luscious chronicles of fully embodied, passionate living?

Future Plans

We must live and be here now in the present moment. For phenomenal health, we must also joyously anticipate our future life.

When I work with folks who are on the quest for miraculous healing, I notice a common thread for supercharging the human body—there needs to be a reason out in the future that they need to live for. This ultimate desire cosmically energizes the cells for invincible recovery!

If you have been riding along in your life, putting one foot in front of the other, you may be operating just above survival. A monumental step for you would be to awaken the dreamer within and allow this dreamer to have their say. Focus on your extraordinary life. Know that you are so blessed and unstoppable.

What are your dreams, goals, and aspirations? Are you exhilarated when you think of these ambitions? If not, get some new dreams! You need to be passionately ecstatic about the road ahead. The only one that's slowing you down is you, so give yourself a big kickstart and create your outrageous impassioned future!

Has Helen Keller said, "Life is a daring adventure or nothing at all!"

YOUR SPIRITUAL LIFE

Feeling yourself connected with the divine, God, the Universe, Universal life force, nature, however you view your higher power, is the brilliant way to keep your cells sparkly and refreshed.

We start with the God of your heart. That may be your high self. The God of your childhood may be a religious figure, perhaps an old man with a beard or a goddess in flowing gowns, and maybe the god of your passions, the nature God, or the Buddha, Christ, or Mohammed. Who or whatever represents the divine is perfect for you!

There is no right way for everyone—just your way for you until you find another.

Whenever I take someone into a meditation or healing, I start with a blessing. May it be with the blessings of the Supreme Being that whatever happens during this healing be a blessing and benefit to each of us in body, mind, and spirit. Amen.

You are connected. You may be oblivious to the fact that divinity and grace are all around you, but there is no denying the force of love and infinite blessings available to each of us as we open our hearts to all good.

Your Secret Keys to Getting Connected with the Divine Connection—Prayer

Both adoration and supplication are superb aspects of connecting with the divine. In prayer, we greet the divine and proceed with all that we are grateful for (adoration) or make our request for love, guidance, and assistance.

Guruji Keshavadas was the guru I studied with during those blissful months in India. He was a round man, short of stature and would often break out into the most enchanting impish grin whenever mischief or humor was at hand. Our life together had many peacefully serene and equally intense, hectic moments. On a rare occasion, we would steal a moment out of the public eye and find time to chat about the mundane world and things related to the health of the body.

When Guruji heard my story of cancer, and the painful divorce I went through, in addition to the outrageously intense devotional life I had led, he came to one conclusion. In his very thick Indian accent, he said, "Vedama (my Indian name), God must love you so very much that he has given you a great deal to pray about. He is a selfish God, and He wants to keep your mind always focused on Him in prayer." Perhaps that is true, for it is so, that I am often in prayer.

I have always prayed, from the traditional Christian prayers I recited as a child, to my own heart's prayer, to the prayers of song, to the Indian Mantra, and doing devotional chanting. When I pray, there is always a presence I sense and always an answer.

Adoration

Adoration is truly and completely the practice of gratitude. As a young girl, my father would escort his little tribe of five unyielding children to the Valley of Peace Lutheran Church. In my eyes, dad was a giant, (5'6"). Things weren't always so cool on the home front, but when dad entered the church, his devotion took over. I was the most cooperative in the bunch when it came to attending church. I was a pipsqueak of a lassie at the tender age of six. My vocal brother, Marty, and sister, Anita, were concerned about their cool image, so it was more than mildly painful to attend church with our "dorky" dad.

We would always sit in a pew close to the front of the church. Pop, who can't carry a tune, (he was tone deaf), and who had no natural rhythm, would burst forth in his passionate out-of-tune voice and sing the songs of adoration to the God of his heart:

"Oh Lord, my God, I am in awesome wonder
when I consider all the worlds Thy hands have made.
I see the stars; I hear the roaring thunder,
Thy power throughout the universe displayed.
Then sings my soul my Savior God to Thee.
How great Thou art, how great Thou art.
Then sings my soul my Savior God to Thee
How great Thou art, how great Thou art!"

Marty and Anita would duck under the pew, hoping nobody would realize that man with the loud out-of-key voice was their dad. I, on the other hand, would stand firm, happy in knowing that Daddy loved God. I felt so happy. I would sing my love and adoration to God also.

Adoration doesn't have to be perfect; it just has to happen. Wire it into your day. Praise God or the Universe in your own special way.

How to Experience Adoration

- Make a gratitude list every morning upon rising.

- Adore and praise your friends and family members.
- See God in each individual. Bless, thank, and share with them those beautiful qualities they are bringing forth.
- Sing songs of celebration and love.
- Read scriptures of adoration, the Psalms, and the Song of Solomon.
- Thank and love the natural environment: Bless the rising and setting sun. Take time to be in awe of a fragrant blooming rose, a cascade of jasmine or a babbling brook.

Supplication

In the prayer of supplication, you earnestly ask for guidance and assistance as you move through your day. Perhaps you are asking for blessings for others who are suffering, or you have met with challenges that are currently beyond your scope to solve alone. Supplication implies you know that you need the assistance of a cosmically charged answer to bring rightness back into a challenging situation.

Forget the concept of "I should be able to figure this out on my own." Do your figuring, but ask the Universe for assistance.

A few years ago, I decided to make God my business partner. It sounds a bit irreverent, but "God" had no objections. And honestly, I have relished the Supreme collaboration! I get empowered by being part of this invincible dynamic duo! I am good, but do sooo much better when I am super-charged with God's love and wisdom! I have a direct line to ask the Divine for assistance and guidance at any moment. We all have it.

Imagine you are learning the game of golf. You understand that you will want to get good equipment, have a club to practice with, and engage in a routine to hone your skills. When you start out, you know your results will be a bit hit or miss and you know it will take some time to produce excellent results. You also know that the more you practice, the sooner that day will come. Slowly, over time, you develop greater skill and more accuracy that yields you better and better results. The more you practice and relax into the process, the greater the ease and better the results become.

Supplication and prayer are like this. You start out as a beginner, and you know that your results may be a bit hit or miss at the beginning. With regular practice, good spiritual tools, and an open heart, you can begin to relax into an incredible connection, a wonderful conversation with the Divine.

If on the other hand, your prayer is like that of a gambler, your emergency pleas may work or fall so far off the mark your request remains unanswered.

Why? The energy vibration of prayers is sometimes so low that it doesn't reach into the realms of miraculous answers. If you are having a tough time, raise your energy vibration before putting in your request for assistance. Walk in nature, play with children, listen to Mozart—you know what brings your vibration up. Know that you are not alone. The Universe is waiting with open arms to shower you with love, abundance, good health, and vitality.

A Call to Lighten

"Soft the night and sweet the spirit,
gentle voices call our song.
We are magic; we are wonder,
when we live beyond the veil.
Humankind, please raise your thoughts.
Bring a plane of peace and love.
We are guardians of the pilgrims,
we the authors of the play."
—Julie Renee, *From Breaking Through,* a book of Poems, 1995

Connection – Meditation

The serene reflection of your spirit to the realm of profound inner peace; this is meditation. There are many versions of meditation. I will describe the three varieties with which I have the most experience.

1. Superb Systematic Focused Clairvoyant Meditation

    This is the style of meditation I teach to my students. We begin with grounding and clearing tools. We progress through steps to bring ease, focus, and vibrant health to the practitioner. This meditation is a lifetime practice. For practice "Meditation Recordings," start with the *Definitive Guide to Meditation* found on my products' page at julierenee.com I provide you with numerous guided meditation programs.

2. The Transformative Yogic Style of Meditation

    This meditation style originates from Mother India. Depending on the teacher or sect of Hinduism, the precise focus of the meditation will slightly shift. However, all of these blissful meditations have a common thread that stitches them together.

    Sitting on the floor cross-legged, ideally, following an integrative Hatha Yoga practice, allow your body to become peaceful. With your spine erect, allow your eyes to fall closed and begin focusing on breathing in and out. As you focus on your breath, begin to repeat your mantra silently to yourself. Repeat you mantra until you have reached a plan of stillness in mind. Sit in the third eye, relaxed and calm, and rest in the silence. Allow passing thoughts to drift away as if they were feathers blowing in the air.

    There are hundreds of mantras. You can experiment with these favorites:

- Om Namah Shivia
- Shree Rama Jai Rama Jai Jai Rama
- Om Gum Ganapatia Namaha

3. Buddhist Walking Meditation

   This form of meditation involves an entirely enjoyable process of conscious prayerful walking, in alignment with your breathing. Each step creates the rhythm and pace of the meditation. This is a beautiful trance walk in which you can experience a heightened awareness of your environment and the blessings that surround you in all directions.

   While studying with Ali Akbar Khan, I learned a beautiful Bengali song, "Suddhi Bisha Ragi." Here is a rough translation:

   "My God, when I look around and open my eyes, I awaken and see all You have given me. My heart is overflowing, and my eyes are filled with tears."

   Taking this practice to the limits is incredible. As a young woman, I became fascinated with the process of oneness with all. While on vacation with my daughter, Britta, age eleven at the time, I had an amazing, blissed out, walking meditation.

   As a preteen and a self-proclaimed couch potato, Britta insisted, "Mom, you go for a walk; I don't want to." Probably too much togetherness, combined with a long road trip and a few extra preteen hormones, spurred me on to take my meditation space while she hung out at the observation area. I figured I would be walking for 20 minutes and would always be in sight; it was a perfect solution for both of us.

   I breathed in and took my first step. Rapidly, I began to melt into everything and become one with the surrounding forest, animals, and pastoral area. My essence became still as I prayerfully put one foot in front of the other while watching the earth beneath my feet. I progressed into a deep trance. Slowly, I began to resurface from my enraptured journey and became aware that my beautiful blond-haired girl was waving her hands and shouting at me.

Hmmm, I wondered why she looked so distressed and was shouting at me. I ran towards her and asked, "Honey, what's wrong?"

"Mom, don't ever do that again!"

Hmmm, what had I done?

"Mom, you walked right up to that buffalo."

"I did?"

We were in Yellowstone Park, which was full of bears, snakes, and the enormous buffalo. I had apparently walked right up to a buffalo. An obnoxious tourist lady bolted towards me, thinking I had been petting the humongous creature. She took after it with her camera pointed. Oooh, I shudder to think about that scene with the charging tourist.

With my daughter's senses heightened and her anxiety up, I was able to share with her: "Honey, when you allow your energy to become one with the environment, you do not register as a threat to the creatures who live there. I was always safe, as my meditation created a peaceful, blissful vortex out of which the only answer was coming to me was a matching vibration." To be in the state of listening to the "all of everything," to be still, is the practice of a lifetime. The rewards from this style of meditation, trust, and oneness are endless and bountiful.

"In the stillness, In the quiet, In the open heart, there I am.
I am essence; I am breath, I am light of God, I am I am."
—Julie Renee, 1991

Connection – The Glory of God in Nature

Beach Time

I love the beach with its exquisite and endless sand and surf. I revel in the glow of the brilliant sun's tenderness, reflecting up from warm sands under bare feet. For me, experiencing the vast infinite expanse of sky and sea is exuberant perfection! I have logged many hours of relaxing ecstasy while blissfully enjoying beach combing.

Think about your moments spent by the ocean or a lake. Remember feeling a sense of well-being and ease? Large bodies of water relate to the still calm waters of the emotional body. Can you remember a feeling of grace flooding over you in your happy memories of beach time? The beachside configuration of protons and electrons brings your positive and negative ions into balance and right order. One of God's little perfect miracles is to spend a day at the beach where your emotional body can comfortably relax, and you can be happy without having to "do anything to fix yourself."

There are many spiritual teaching related to the ocean. There is the concept of the "ocean of mercy," "Mary of the Sea," and the "ocean of bliss."

Hawaii is jammed-packed with beaches galore. While I was visiting Maui, the warm, gentle rains of the afternoon misted the lush forest. Very sweetly, rain drops laid themselves into the ocean. As one drop fell into the infinite expanse, it became one with everything. We are like the raindrops. When the drop falls into the deep blue sea it knows itself; when it merges into the sea, it knows the vast expanse. Knowledge and wisdom of the known universe now become easily accessible and available.

If you listen carefully, you can hear the voice of God in the crashing waves and the abandoned seashells. As you look out over the open sea and experience the unending brilliance of the painted sky, you can feel blissfully connected with the Divine.

In India, I learned a special practice to do by the ocean as the sun rises or sets. Take your mala (prayer beads) in hand as you gaze at the horizon line. Chant or repeat the mantra for enlightenment below, or use your personal mantra. The practice of reciting prayers while observing the rising or setting sun as it makes its way under or over the horizon line is a yogic practice. Implementing this method amplifies your prayers one hundred fold. I have spent many evenings with prayer beads in hand, gazing off into the horizon as the sun is setting while saying the mantra for enlightenment.

"Om Bu buva swaha om tat savitur varenium bargo devasya dimahi diyoyo naha prochodiat."

* Translation is not literal but the feeling of:
Oh God! Thou art the Giver of Life,
Remover of pain and sorrow,
The Bestower of happiness,
Oh! Creator of the Universe,
May we receive thy supreme sin-destroying light,
May Thou guide our intellect in the right direction

The seaside visits are thought of when convalescing and when returning and restoring oneself to vibrant health. The rhythmic healing waves rush to the beach and disappear into the hungry sands. At water's edge the seagull, pelican, tern and sandpiper make their indelible imprint on the mind of the observer.

Hiking in the Wilderness

Nature is an exhilarating experience for restoring the body to peace and ease and for expanding our sense of well-being and connection.

HOW TO BE UNSTOPPABLE IN YOUR MEDITATION PRACTICE

1. Avoid the "hurried, scattered, grab a few minutes here or there" approach when beginning your meditation practice. When starting a practice that will benefit you for a lifetime, you need to make a commitment. Find a regular time each day, regardless of other demands or priorities, where you can devote time to your spiritual growth. This may mean you wake up earlier every day to meditate for twenty minutes before the kids are stirring or routine responsibilities are calling. Or perhaps your best time happens before bed or during lunch. Consider what is best for you and commit to it for 90 days; adjust your time if necessary, but honor your promise to yourself. Give yourself a high level of permission to enjoy and experience your personal and spiritual growth.
2. Avoid meditating in an ungrounded or busy space. Find a spot (in your home or garden preferably) where you will meditate every day. The energy of this space needs to be

dedicated to your spiritual pursuits, and it needs to be a space that is calming. You can still fulfill your daily practice when traveling. Carry a meditation cushion or a 12"x18" piece of white wool, which will become infused with your energy, and remember to ground and own the room for yourself.

3. Avoid eating a big meal just prior to meditation. Oops! Food in the tummy is a big distraction. A common practice, if you feel you need nourishment, is to have a cup of chai or a small amount of fresh fruit, so you remain in the bliss zone. Heavy meals will draw the blood and Prana (life force energy) out of your head and into your lower chakras. Meditation is about lifting up into the upper chakras and enjoying the seven chakras above your head. It is so much fun when all the energies are in sync!

4. Avoid sitting in an uncomfortable position, feeling chilled, or allowing yourself too warm. Intentionally create a beautiful, simple space. Experienced yogis and yoginis enjoy a meditation shawl and cushion. But it is just as appropriate to sit upright in a chair with a cozy afghan wrap. Remember, these are dedicated moments of special connection with your Sacred Self. Give yourself permission to be completely comfortable and feel supported. When dealing with chronic pain, and in this case only, a lying down meditation is a good choice. I don't recommend this posture for others because lying down is the position for sleep. Of course, sleep is wonderful and necessary, but that is not the goal of meditation. Those who choose the lying down form must be extra diligent to stay present and alert.

5. Avoid self-criticism and "perfect pictures." Ouch! These are the pictures of having to be perfect, get it right, or expecting to be an expert immediately or during every meditation

session. If you tell yourself you can't meditate, then you will fulfill that command. But let me reassure you that everyone can meditate. It's like exercising a muscle—the more often you work out, the stronger your muscles get. Likewise, the more you practice meditation (the key word here is practice, not perfect), the more reliable and easier your practice will become. Remind yourself that you are in a learning/adapting phase and that you love the sacred time spent in meditation. I provide you with beautiful guidance on the meditation tapes. Within a few days or weeks, you will remember all the steps, and then we can enhance your personalized meditation program.

Relax, enjoy, and have fun. This is not serious stuff. It is the fuel for bliss, happiness, and deep connection with yourself, the God of your heart, and all others! How wonderful for you to have come to a place in your journey where you can receive this gift of self-love, care, and awareness!

YOUR LIFE IN BALANCE

There are eight essential elements to living your life in balance. You will experience your life in a profound state of satisfaction and ease when you embrace these necessary fundamentals and keep them in a fulfilled state.

Often when your life is off-kilter, you have put all of your energies into just a couple areas on the balance wheel.

It's also fun to see that you can take your life back. When you become responsible for how your life shows up for you, and you bring just a little more satisfaction into each area of your life, you will begin to feel powerful beyond measure and truly unstoppable.

Two years ago, Sharon started doing life coaching sessions with me. She was an American-born, Asian woman with very traditional Asian parents. She had made a mark for herself in the New York fashion industry but had decided to return to San Francisco to spend time with her aging parents. She had a few personality quirks that she was embarrassed about, and Sharon often found herself being critical and judgmental: "I have all the money I need," she'd say, "but I spend so much money on clothes I don't care about." Her life was unsatisfying, and she honestly didn't know why.

We began working on the balance wheel, which will be explained in depth shortly. At the same time, I suggested Sharon read *The Four Agreements* by Don Miguel Ruiz. What we discovered was that she felt without meaning or purpose in her life. She questioned her career, her friends, and her entire lifestyle.

Gently, we worked the balance wheel together. Step-by-step, she committed to making small changes and shifts. These changes continued to bring her satisfaction and joy in each area. She began an extensive training as a yoga instructor. Her friends started changing; some old friendships faded away while some healthy new ones emerged. She implemented new meaningful practices in her daily routines. Sharon was waking up from the sleep of an unconscious lifestyle. She was making significant choices to be the captain of her ship, rather than let the currents take her wherever a rudderless life goes.

When Sharon graduated from her coaching experience, she emanated joy and peace. The aspect of her personality that was frustrated and judgmental had calmed down, and her love and gratitude vibe had significantly expanded. "I had no idea how unhappy I was," she told me. Her life had turned around 180 degrees. She was now embracing a future of intimate friendships, purposeful livelihood, and a new energy signature in the love vibration!

In these next few pages, you will discover the secret of a genuine and profound happiness. This information is priceless. Don't be fooled by the simplicity of the process. This is the answer to being content and experiencing a fully self-expressed life.

Grab a marker and a piece of paper. Draw a circle, and divide that circle into a pie with eight segments. In the upper right section, write "Social and Friends."

Name:_____

Date:_____

Wheel diagram with eight segments labeled: Health/Recreation, Social/Friends, Emotional, Career, Family/Friends, Finance, Spirituality, Creativity/Dance/Art/Music

ELEMENT ONE—
BALANCE SOCIAL AND FRIENDS

Let your mind search through your recent history. Bring into focus the sense you have of your social life. When you think about your social life, are you feeling fulfilled and happy? Are you connected with friends who are positive and fun? Do you feel like you are often in your tribe—the social group where you feel like a pea in the pod? Get a percentage of satisfaction level in your mind For example, "very happy and fulfilled" might be 90% or 100%, while "very little satisfaction" might be 10% or 20%.

Does your social life have a place of prominence? Are you making sure you are having some relaxed, carefree moments as you go through your week? Living life in balance requires that you have an excellent relationship with your friends. Statistics show that we age better when we have a sense of connection in community.

Why is it important to have a social life? We, as humans, were meant to experience relaxation and joy in the body. Our bodies gain courage and strength from those comfortable, happy times.

Those happy moments are the emotional fortification we need for when tough times arrive. You can weather stress and challenge with little interruption to equanimity when your emotional bank of happy moments is well-stocked.

What is your social behavior policy? Are you set for relaxed, happy moments several times a week when you are out in the world? Do you feel the importance of this activity? Some families have a policy related to working hard whereby self-sacrifice is emphasized, or social pleasure is denied unless it is well earned. If you have come from this patterning, you may not realize that working in overdrive and placing your social activities at the bottom of the list may affect you in the most adverse ways.

Some problems that might show up if you are ignoring your social life include:

- Being over critical of family members and self
- Lacking constructive communication styles
- Being overly self-identified
- Having a short temper
- Feeling depressed
- TV addiction
- Lung and digestive problems

Signs of having a good balanced social life include:

- Feeling a sense of connection
- Having support
- Experiencing camaraderie
- Having a good sense of humor, laughing easily
- Resilience in trying times
- Satisfaction levels with self and outer life significantly increases

Do you reside in your happy life with a good balance of play time with friends?

Draw a line in the first segment of your wheel that identifies your satisfaction level at the present moment. If it is satisfaction at 100%, you will be following the outside eclipse with the outer edge of the pie

Balance in this area does not mean that you are doing things with your friends around the clock, seven days a week. Although satisfaction levels are unique to each, a good guide for testing if you are in the ballpark for living life in social balance would mean you are spending about 10%-20% of your time enjoying your life with other people.

What you are looking for is personal satisfaction. Anyone can raise their satisfaction level to 100% over a period of weeks. If you are feeling a bit weak in this area, you can create some action steps to elevate your contentment point. Here is a short list of activities you can do to develop deeper levels of connection and ease.

- Meet a girlfriend for tea
- Hook up with a buddy for mountain biking
- Throw a dinner party and invite folks you'd like to get to know better
- Catch a baseball game with friends
- Rally friends for a night of dancing
- Join a Meet Up group focused on your favorite special interest
- Plan a monthly "Girls Night Out" and catch a romantic comedy
- Invite your musician friends over to jam in your living room
- Go camping with other families or friends from school
- Assemble a group for lunch at a new restaurant
- Plan a spa day with a few close friends
- Watch a game with your friends at a sports bar

- Attend a spiritual event and circulate
- Go to a concert or ballet with associates
- Plan a beach day or picnic with the ones you love and bring a Frisbee

Create a plan involving less activity if you are in the minority of folks who are overly active and addicted to going out. Develop your filter for experiencing high-quality activities while reducing your overall number of events. This selectivity will bring your satisfaction level up. When you are overly busy with social activities, you will find your satisfaction level to be low because you are over-stretched. We need movement and rest. Too much of a good thing is not okay either. If you are on overdrive with your social life, take a look at where you are getting the good stuff from, and leave out the activities that waste your time.

ELEMENT TWO—
BALANCE YOUR EMOTIONAL BODY

The second segment in the balance wheel is the category for the emotional body. 100% satisfaction in the emotional category reflects your feelings of living a blessed life whereby you are often in bliss and are feeling so grateful for everything that comes to you. You have a sense of love and anticipation for the wonder and goodness of life, and you live in a gentle flow of grace and ease.

Are you mostly in the state of bliss? Are you content? Connected with the Divine? Do you feel that all is well in the universe?

Let yourself get in touch with your feeling body. Reach out with your thoughts into the recent past. What were the recurring feelings that surfaced for you through this past week?

On the low end of the emotional segment is sadness, melancholy, depression, and anxiety. At the extremely low ebb, we find "bottom of the barrel" emotions—thoughts of suicide, ongoing pain and anger, jealousy, and unrelenting self-criticism. Sometimes folks get so sad they just wonder if life is worth living. If you find yourself in the lower range, it is time to start taking some action to improve your happiness and satisfaction levels.

Pick a number for yourself. There is a big range in emotional contentment and ease. If you are under 50%, you will find that there is something else on the wheel that is also out of balance. Maybe it's creativity. Perhaps you are not spending enough time painting or dancing. Or maybe the balance is off concerning your finances or recreation. When you desire true abundance, your emotional segment needs to be pretty rockin'.

To get your feelings into a preferred emotional range of over 75% satisfaction:

- Let yourself notice all the good you have in your life
- Stop talking about the poor behaviors of others
- Start talking about how loved and lucky you are!
- Keep a gratitude journal
- Create a bulletin board of all your happy adventures, or all the beautiful cards you receive from those you love
- Send a love letter to an older relative, and let them know how much their life and examples have meant to you
- Volunteer at a soup kitchen or shelter
- Be a Big Brother or Sister or adopt a grandparent
- Get out in nature, hike with a friend, go mountain biking, or take a ski trip
- Babysit and have fun getting into the playfulness of life
- Forgive everyone
- Forgive yourself
- Plan a journey around the world
- Go dancing
- Dress up
- Turn off the TV

- Avoid violence
- Avoid sensational news and radio shows
- Listen to classical or mellow music
- Watch a romantic comedy or an excellent documentary
- Find reasons to laugh. (The average child finds 300 occasions a day to laugh while the average adult laughs three times or less; kick up your laughing quotient.)
- Light some candles
- Enjoy a fresh bouquet of flowers
- Spend time in prayer and meditation
- Journal

Helpful Supports for When Action Is Not Enough

If you have been in a low vibe for a long time, get a neurotransmitter test. Find out if your serotonin and dopamine levels are sufficiently high. You can take natural neurotransmitter supports from NeuroScience Labs www.neurorelief.com

Our brain regeneration VIP program addresses the neurotransmitters beautifully, and you can use the quantum pump to continue to boost your neurotransmitters daily if you choose to! Please refer to *Your Divine Human Blue Print* book which is the guide to regeneration. You can find it online and on our website.

Alternative Products to Improve Brain Chemistry:

- Essential oils including grapefruit, tangerine, and mandarin quell anxiety and stimulate productivity. I like Amrita Oils.
- Use Sam-E, St. John's Wort, Rescue Calm, and Field of Flowers (from Energetix)
- If you are prone to mood swings, look into balancing your hormones. Use my *Happy Hormones* CD to tune up your entire endocrine system (for women and men).

- Experiment with these herbs: Black Cohosh, Evening Primrose, Borage Oil, DHEA, and Wild Yam Extract

One of the surefire ways to raise your satisfaction in this area is to start loving yourself the way you are. Praise and bless yourself for the little steps you are making. Sometimes it takes courage and discipline to transcend an old pattern. You can do it. Remember a time when you rose to the occasion and took a stand for yourself against all the odds? Remember how good it felt then? Use these positive memories to fuel your steps upward toward pleasure and ease.

I encourage you to be a scientific researcher in the area of emotions and get to your happy space. Take little steps and be firmly focused on the happiness that is coming in for you. Fortify this area for real peace.

ELEMENT THREE—
BALANCE CAREER

Just under the midline on the right side of the Balance Wheel is Career. 0% is dismal. If you are there, you are most likely feeling hopelessly lost. On the other hand, if you are at 100% you are working your dream job, making all the money your heart desires. The middle range is where you find some satisfaction in your career, but you are not yet feeling aligned with your higher soul's purpose or calling.

Slow and steady wins the race when raising the bar for your career. Wherever you find yourself, claim that you are on your way and that you are just looking for ways to help your career become more embodied. If you are under 50%, definitely give your energy to this. *Book Yourself Solid* by coach and author Michael Port, is a great book to help you on that path and get you on that rocking career.

When thinking about attaining deep satisfaction in your career, your first step is feeling happy about your present calling. Think about what you are doing right now. What do you love about it?

Why did you choose this position over all other choices? Do you enjoy the environment? The people you work with? Your boss? Do you look forward to the tasks at hand? What areas of implementation at work do you enjoy?

When you start bringing your life into balance, we don't want you to blast your life apart. We are looking for you to bring more satisfaction slowly into your life. Eventually, you might graduate to a career that you have a passion for, but raising the energy vibration of your relationship to your current work allows you to bring in your real and fulfilling life's passion.

- How could you bring more satisfaction to this area?
- Do you feel you are the best at what you do?
- If you do not yet feel you are the best at what you do ~What do you need to shift to make that last statement true
- How can you serve your clients better?
- How can you improve on fulfillment?
- Are you impeccable with your word?
- How can you contribute to the folks you work with in extraordinary ways?
- If earning large amounts of money will add to your pleasure and satisfaction, what steps do you need to take to make that happen?

If you aren't in a high level of satisfaction in this area, you only have you to answer to. At any moment you can change your mind and create a new thrilling livelihood for the fulfillment of your soul's calling.

ELEMENT FOUR— FAMILY AND FRIENDS

Your relationship with the ones you love is such an important factor in creating a healthy, vibrant abundant life! Rate your satisfaction in this area by measuring your level of ease and peace with your intimate family and friends. 0% represents feeling totally disconnected and disappointed; you are possibly angry or unresolved around how you thought your life should have gone when you were young. If you are on this end of the scale, you are most likely finding yourself stuck in your ability to be happy in your personal relationships in general. You also have not yet been able to release the past and take responsibility for how things are at this moment.

    100% means that you are in love with your life and are content with the way you hold your relationships. 100% is feeling over the moon, loved and cherished, and fully in your happy place. It does not mean you have to be in love with what might have happened to you in the past, but that you have now resolved the issues to the point where you know your life is in divine order from your family. Think of this section as to how you relate to your tribe—not necessarily your family—but the people who you love and cherish.

On the low end of the scale regarding your family and friends, you will find that the unresolved issues of your past affect your present time relationships. If you have done a lot of therapy, or personal growth work around these unresolved issues, holding onto the past may actually be a spiritual, or energetic issue. If that is the case, it is not resolvable from mental work, i.e. through talking and thinking.

When you have a relationship—any relationship—contacts are formed, agreements are made, energetic chords are plugged in, energy is exchanged, and perhaps karma has been generated between you and the other person.

I have developed spiritual healing techniques to clear these entanglements that will bring you to neutrality.

I was working with a wonderful client, Joyce, who was recovering from Lyme disease, as well as an anxiety disorder. She had three young girls, was in her mid-thirties, and had left the Mormon faith to marry. She was such a light and was so courageous.

One of the issues that would loop through our healing sessions concerned her family relationships, and the discord and disharmony, especially between her parents and her. Both had divorced and had remarried. To assist her in healing her anxiety and restore her vibrant health, we proceeded to clear all energetic entanglements that she had with her parents and her brothers and sisters.

This clearing happened in perfect timing. Just prior to the clearing, she had traveled to see her family and had experienced a very difficult interaction with them. However, after the clearing, she returned to her family for her grandmother's birthday celebration. (Just as a side note I had also been working with her younger sister, though she was not apprised of the clearing we had done for her older sis.)

No short of miraculous, the whole family had received the healing! For the first time ever, all of the family members got along beautifully with one another. Chrissie her little sister, called me after the fact to find out if I had anything to do with this phenomenon.

She told me: "It was an absolute miracle, Julie Renee. Everyone was talking to each other. We actually let our guard down and were really enjoying each other!"

SPIRITUAL EMOTIONAL—ENTANGLEMENTS AND HOW TO CLEAR THEM

Spiritual Emotional ~ Entanglements and How to Clear Them

Contracts

A spiritual contract is an agreement you have unconsciously or consciously made that does not go away until it is fulfilled. You could have said, "Let's grow old together." Or the contract could have been implied. For example, you always knew that your mother expected you as the oldest daughter to stay with her and take care of her in her old age. So, there are spoken and implied contracts, and both can weigh heavily on you until they are cleared.

Agreements

Very much like contracts, your agreements are things that you agreed to. These things may no longer have any validity, but they may still play out. For example, you might have agreed to be ruled by the voice of guilt, which would always curtail your full enjoyment of life or a particular area of your life.

Energetic Chords

The first way we experience chords is when we connect in with our little bodies as a newly forming embryo. We first chord into our own little body, and by the time birth takes place, we are well-chorded to our mothers, and perhaps our fathers. Chords are a lifeline for us at this point. Mothers are often said to have a sixth sense. A lot of times, this "sense" is actually because of the open chord, which allows a clear flow of information to mommy about the safety and comfort of her baby.

Since this chording worked out for you as an infant, it often becomes a habit to chord into the ones you are close to. It is part of our human nature. However, we really don't need to be chorded into anyone once we reach the age of decision and discernment. Left over chords often need conscious unplugging to be fully completed and cleared.

Energy Exchange

When you feel a strong emotion, your energy goes into the person who you are having that feeling about. Whether it be love or hate, tenderness or anger, with strong emotions, energy from you goes into them and vice versa. I use a "spiritual magnet" to pull all the energy out of each of you and return the energy to its original owner. If you are no longer being treasured and have become somewhat invisible in your relationship, for example, try magnetizing your energy out of your partners. This really works in most cases. When you have too much energy in someone else's body, they no longer experience you as a separate individual.

Karma

Karma includes all the entanglements from this lifetime and all your past entanglements from previous lives that were generated between you and your loved one. The bottom line is that we cycle through lifetimes in which we create unresolved issues. We come back together in the hopes that we will get it right. Sometimes we do naturally complete our karma, but more often than not, we just add to the list of unresolved problems to fix in some future life.

There is a meditation tool that clears this "karma" permanently! If you would like to discover more about removing energetic entanglements, you will find several excellent resources on my website including: "The Definitive Guide To Karma Clearing," the Unlimited Love Special Event, and the Monthly Secret Keys audio series. www.Julierenee.com

ELEMENT FIVE—FINANCE

The next category is finance. This category includes everything needed in order for you to be financially balanced and secure. It feels wonderful to have good cash flow, and to earn enough to support your healthy lifestyle. But often, folks forget the other essential ingredients for being fiscally wise and monetarily sound.

My youthful self was dynamically entrepreneurial. In high school, I had multiple streams of income. I earned money from babysitting, sewing bow ties for the boys in the Select and Chamber choir, and I worked as a hostess at Burger King. In my teens, I always had extra cash to lend my sisters when they needed a few extra dollars. I had a hope chest of treasured gifts from the money I'd saved to take with me into a marriage.

When I was quite young, at age 18, I married a farmer. As the years went by, we struggled financially with the family farm. The lifestyle of daily chores and field work was an honorable and sacred path, but our money life was dismal. I went seven years without buying a new dress or new shoes. My father would say, "He may not have much money, but he is a hard worker."

These were hard times and love was rarely present—just struggle and survival. I sewed clothes for our children, and the neighbors were always more than generous with hand-me-downs and extra food from their gardens; so somehow we got by.

By the time I divorced at age 24, I was a young and very sick mother of three. I was ill-equipped to understand the big picture concerning creating financial security. But through a series of mistakes, I learned how to proceed and create a sound financial picture.

Mistake number one: After I secured two part-time jobs—working at Kentucky Fried Chicken, as well as the North Hennepin Community College library on a work study program—I filled out forms for a credit card! I had no furniture to speak of or home supplies to furnish my little apartment. So, I got myself set up with a number of credit cards.

Oh my gosh, was that fun for a couple months! I bought what I needed and maxed out the cards. On the little money I was earning, I had no way to repay the debts. Ugggh. After some time of phone calls and making small payments, I landed better jobs—waitressing at a classy Mexican Restaurant (Estebans in Anoka Minnesota), and a graphic design internship with the Minneapolis Police Department.

Slowly, I chipped away at the unrelenting bills. But the weight of the debt caused me to feel over-alert and anxious. I don't remember feeling happy or content back then.

During my college years, I also had relied on the medical program available for students. I drove a wreck of a car and had minimal insurance. I had a checking account, but no savings. Fortunately, when I graduated from college and went to work selling real estate, I was able to round out the picture a bit better.

However, my learning curve and improvements to my fiscal health was a long and winding road. I came to teach about abundance out of a real need to generate abundance, regardless of my outer circumstances. My early career as a farm wife, student, realtor, and healer was smattered with endless health challenges. Days, weeks, and sometimes years off of work to recover from surgeries, (in addition to a serious accident), wreaked havoc on my bank account.

When I was working, I would gain momentum and begin the catch-up process, only to fall again in which my body would go into another health recovery cycle.

I have always felt blessed and have somehow made ends meet, but actually, I was homeless at age 34 for one year. That was the year I housesat, and slept in the back of my station wagon when I had no housesitting gigs. I needed to find a way to consistently bring in abundance, and as you know, abundance isn't necessarily money; it could be a living situation, or food, or loving friends.

I sought out to discover how I could be a living, vital magnet for all good. I studied in India and learned the chants to remove debt and manifest income. I read books on Feng Shui and learned how to transform my home and my spirit towards attracting all good. I also learned about meditation techniques to magnetize abundance and all excellence to me.

Unless you are very fortunate or have been trained in how to have a healthy financial life from your parents of teachers, you may have also learned from the mistakes and pressures of living in a plastic culture. Earning money is only one component of a complex picture for experiencing a dynamically successful life. Let's take a look at the other items you will want to put in place to round out the picture:

1. **Income** from work or other sources—preferably multiple streams of income.
2. A conscious, functioning **Budget**, and if you are currently in debt, a **debt repayment plan**.

3. **Two Savings accounts**—one for planned spending, such as things that are not included in your monthly budget, but that you know will come up during the year; and the second is your security account. This should include six months of savings in case you choose to take some time off or need to not work for some other unexpected reason.
4. **Retirement fund** and a **retirement plan**—even if you don't plan to "retire." We are looking both for funds in a 401k or IRA and a written plan of what you are intending to do after age 70 (or earlier).
5. **Will and Trust, Durable Power of Attorney, and Health Care Directive**
6. **Insurance**: Home Owners, Renters, Car, Health care, Disability, Life.
7. **Home ownership** or savings towards home ownership.
8. **Read** a minimum of two good financial books a year to keep up-to-date with changing trends.
9. **Teach your children** to do these steps and pass the legacy of financial abundance onto generations to come!

To be brilliant with your finances, and to be able to say with great conviction, "I am unbelievably blessed in my financial life," you need to embody the space of impeccability and honor.

The financial programming I grew up with went something like this: "You don't need to know the ins and outs of the complete financial picture; a man will do this part of your life." I have struggled for years to get beyond that program and enjoy the aspects of wealth and abundance that I so ecstatically live.

Four years ago I started affirming:

I am a Financial Genius and a Master of Money! Everything I touch turns to GOLD. I live in Divine flow. All goodness comes to me in Divine right order.

If you are just starting to consider these concepts, I would suggest choosing a good book to guide you as you uncover your Inner Money Master! I personally love Suze Orman's style and her variety of skillfully written books and programs that can help you take charge of your money. Start by implementing each step yourself. You can always tweak your information with a sound financial counselor, bookkeeper or accountant later on, but if you learn how to apply these things first by yourself, you will be unstoppable; you will understand the foundation from which you can fortify your financial life yourself. You can't be successful in building a skyscraper without a solid foundation, so if you are interested in playing big with money, learn these concepts well.

On an energetic level, I would encourage you to purchase the book, *Feng Shui for Abundance*, by David Daniel Kennedy. It took me four months to fully integrate all the shifts in my home and work space that Daniel Kennedy recommended, and I am so happy I did. My financial flow and ease dramatically shifted. You can find this book and Suze Orman's book on my web page. www.JulieRenee.com/resources

Getting your money "right" gives you a chance to soar. You can be a real philanthropist. Having integrity with money allows you the freedom to travel, own the home and car you want, and to live with freedom in your retirement years.

On your wheel, find your level of satisfaction based on the completion of the bullet points listed above. 100% means you have it all handled and 0% says the situation looks dismal.

ELEMENT SIX— SPIRITUALITY

Naturally, this is one of my favorite sections of the wheel. Spirituality, and feeling connected to the Divine, seems to be built into my nature. I love meditation, prayer, studying about many paths to the Divine, and the devotional path to being present to the Divine.

Spirituality—100% is the feeling of really rockin' and experiencing your connection with the Divine. For some, this may mean going to church, or having a regular meditative practice, etc. Zero percent is the feeling that you are blocked in your connection with the Divine.

I have always loved God. In my childhood, the God of my heart was Jesus. I was raised in a traditional German Lutheran home in Minnesota. We prayed at the table and had daily scripture reading. I spent so much time at the Holy Nativity Lutheran Church, it was like my second home. My pastor, Pastor Pete (Ronald Peterson), was my mentor. He was a charismatic preacher who loved serving God. His compelling message packed the pews to the brim.

Eventually, chairs had to be added, and finally, people stood outside the door to hear his sermons. I read my Bible daily and breathed the word of God in my heart.

When I married at 18, I continued my intense activity in the church and became a youth counselor. I also participated in the choir, women's circles, and became a Sunday, school teacher. I loved the activities of the church, and I loved the God of my Heart.

When I became terminally ill, my life was turned upside down: It had become clear to me that the dysfunctional dynamics in my marriage were unhealthy, and that a large contributing factor for the breakdown of my health had to do with the profound unhappiness I had experienced in that union. Despite my belief at the time that divorce was an unforgivable sin, after painful consideration, I did leave my husband. As soon as I filed for divorce, I was asked to leave my church.

The pain of that day affected me for years. But the blessing hidden in the event revealed itself a few years later. As a spirit seeker, I could not stay away from the love of God, so I found unique ways to feel the presence of the Divine.

I had many "out of the box" kinds of experiences that led me to my continued spiritual questing and transformation. I discovered the Aquarian Light Church, the Lake Harriet Community Church and the Unity Church. My heart began to heal and open. I was no longer on the single track of one religion; my spiritual path had started to open in ways I could not have predicted. I also began to travel to South Fallsburg, New York to sit with Gurumayi at her ashram.

Then the door opened fully wide and I stepped through the precipice to my awakening: I found myself on a spiritual pilgrimage in India, traveling with a holy man, learning the ways of a

Pujari (priestess). I studied with the young Brahmin priests and learned Vedic scripture—a rite reserved only for men.

I shifted from my youthful experience of finding God through organized religion, to the expansive experience of the Mystical all and ever presence of Divinity. I did not become a Hindu. Instead, I expanded my awareness to reach higher to the cosmic oneness of all and everything. I was no longer trapped in a belief structure. I had moved to a gloriously free and open exploration of all the beautiful ways humankind experiences the Divine. As a result, the world became simpler and divinity could be experienced now in every moment!

To Have a Healthy Spiritual Life—Simple and Easy

- Pray and meditate daily.
- Be connected with others in a spiritual community.
- Practice kindness and generosity of thought
- Have an "attitude of gratitude" for all things.
- Bonus: Make God your partner!

ELEMENT SEVEN—
CREATIVITY, ART, MUSIC, DANCE

Creativity, Art, Music, and Dance comprise the next segment on the Balance Wheel. These forms of creative expression are food for your soul.

You, as a being, need to create. We were created in the image of God—Creator; we have the gift of creating if we maintain an open creative channel. In your physical body, you have creative channels running from your heart, and flowing through your shoulders, arms, hands and out your fingertips. These channels can stayed tuned up and open by creating.

The creative chakras are the second and fifth chakras. The second chakra is about creating on a physical level, and it includes the miraculous process of pregnancy and birth. It is from this chakra that our physical projects are made manifest.

Projects from the Second Chakra include, but are not limited to:
- Painting
- Sculpture

- Dance
- Gardening
- Creative cooking
- Home decorating
- Playing an instrument
- Sewing
- Beading
- Embroidery
- Carpentry
- Wood carving
- Basket weaving
- Jewelry making
- Ceramics
- Stage design
- Pottery and clay works
- Print making, lithographs
- Hand bookbinding
- Making handmade paper
- Quilting
- Crocheting
- Drawing, doodling, sketching
- Stained glass

The Fifth Chakra is the chakra of communication. Creative expression from this chakra includes:
- Poetry
- Creative writing
- Storytelling
- Opera singing

- Vocal presentation
- Inspirational speaking and reading aloud

To turbo-charge your ability to manifest in the spiritual realm, you need to incorporate your "Creator-God-In-Training" status. Creation is the way in which you express yourself beautifully.

Creating is God's gift of healing through our essence. Leaving the mind out of the equation, we move that which has settled in our body out. Think about a time when you were in the zone of creativity. What did you create? What did you release? What did you realize?

In my spiritual life coaching practice, I occasionally hear: "Oh, I used my creativity to design a new accounting system." Although this may be a form of mental creativity, the kind of creativity that will keep your channels open must keep your joy factor high.

By doing a little joyful activity every week, you will notice a sense of well-being in your essence. This is because creativity gets you into a relaxed flow and into a state of being where your mind is not badgering you to pay attention to all the things that regularly call you away from your essence. Happy endorphins are released into your body's chemistry, and you feel what you were meant to feel and enjoy—a happy, calm body.

Please don't stress. If you are not a naturally creative person, only one hour a week of creative activity will suffice. This is not a full-time requirement, unless this is your career. If you are enjoying an hour or two a week doing something creative, that counts. That's good.

That might be enough to provide the satisfaction you need; others may require more.

Creative expression is one thing my students often think they can let go of on the Balance Wheel and still succeed. Creativity is the frosting on the cake of your life. The cake may be okay without the frosting, but when you add just the right amount, it becomes oh so very sweet and delicious.

If your emotional life is a little out of whack, it may be because you are not enjoying enough creative expression and your creative channels are blocked.

Rate your creative expression. 0% means you experience no creative expression, and 100% means you are content and reaping the benefits of a healthy creative flow.

ELEMENT EIGHT—
HEALTH AND RECREATION

The final segment on the Balance Wheel is health and recreation. Included in this section are the components that comprise a healthy lifestyle. This section reflects your commitment to living your life in a healthy, happy body with great ease and vibrant wellness. The four key players that will be expanded upon below are:

- Ecstatic exercise
- Nourishing nutrition
- Captivating vacations
- Rejuvenating rest

When I refer to ecstatic exercise, I am referring to a way of moving your body that brings you joy! When I was in recovery from my accident, I chose to do restorative yoga in my bed. Having always loved yoga, this was a natural joyful experience for me. Now that I have vibrant health, I love working out with the Power 90 Extreme program, and I run 20 miles a week. There is no right way, just your way until you find another.

Create a lifestyle that supports you in staying fit and healthy. Stretching, cardio, and strength training add up to an unbeatable routine for an extraordinary life.

Nourishing Nutrition

Feed your body with life-giving foods and nutritional supplements that support your energy, vitality, and strength. There are many beautiful, healthful ways to eat. I loved reading the *Slow Down Diet*. This was not a diet. Rather, it promoted a peaceful way of enjoying one's meals, while allowing your body to celebrate the nutrition you are providing it.

I often recommend the *Fat Flush* book. It promotes an alkaline style of cleansing when the body is in need of a break from the rigors of restaurant food and "low vibration" food, such as processed foods.

When thinking about nutrition, remember that everything you feed your body is a source of nutrients or a source of stress. Food is obviously nutrition—it is what we think of when we think of sustenance. Additionally, what we gift our five senses with is also nutrition. As I sit here at my desk writing, I am aware of the essential oil, pink grapefruit, I have distilling in my aromatherapy diffuser. The subtle scent is uplifting and supports great productivity and mental focus. Just to the left of that is a small brass figurine of a dancing Lord Ganesha, who in Hindu mythology, dispels all obstacles. I have books that inspire me placed behind Ganesha, with bright pink orchids and fresh red and plum-colored roses from the garden in my line of sight.

Feeding the five senses with lovely and joyous nutrition is as important, or more important, than physical food. We are feeding the cells. In the book, *The Secret Life of Your Cells*, Cleve Backster, the author, reports his findings of incredible intelligence and memory in the cells of the human body. Dr. Masaru Emoto's research on water molecules reiterates how responsive water molecules are to words, thoughts, sound and music. The implications of Dr. Emoto's research are utterly mindboggling when you consider the human body is over 90% water. Our cells actually become brighter and happier when we feed them beautiful thoughts, scents, sounds, flavors and loving touch.

Captivating Vacations

When you are excited about life and what the future holds, you live a blessed life. Do you currently have a vacation on the schedule?

Think about the times before you went on vacation. The thought of the adventure made the little stressors of life dissipate and become meaningless. Think about times of stress where you felt no end in sight—no vacation planned—just constant stress. Got the picture?

When you are creating fun moments in the work of your daily life, you are creating a way to maintain and support your long-term, vibrant physical health.

As I write this book, I have set aside two weeks for beach vacationing in sunny Mexico.

What is super fantastic is to build a lifestyle of vacationing into every day of your life. There is a great little kit from Debbie Ford, "The Best Year of Your Life," that when followed, makes every day a holiday.

If you are in a time in your life where you are in an accomplishment cycle, and you wish to move and change the world through your contribution, remember to ground your vacations by putting them in your schedule and booking them. You will notice a sense of joy and anticipation. In tough moments, these memories and future happenings will alter the perception of your thoughts. It will allow your body to know that you love it and are scheduling time to take care of it, love it, and let it rest.

There Are Four Kinds of Vacations:

1. Beach bumming, relaxing. On your relaxation vacation, you go to one place, drop your clothes in a heap, and stay put for the duration. You enjoy the slowed down pace of restoration. I do this kind of vacation regularly in Nuevo Vallarta, Mexico and at my fabulous Villa Del Palmar Flamingos time share.

2. Exploration. This is the type of vacation where you are adventuring. It could be a cruise, or a trip to an exotic land, mountain climbing, or going on a pilgrimage. You are in movement and logging in many sites, historical data, and allowing the body to experience the joy of living on Planet Earth. I have taken this type of vacation many times. One of my all-time favorites was traveling through India and touring the temples and holy places for half a year. This kind of holiday changes your life. Coming back from having given yourself this incredible gift, you are richer and wiser for the experience and will now have abundant materials to enhance your strong, healthy, emotional and mental wellbeing.

3. Local short reboot trips. Going to the wine country or a B&B for a couple of days is an amazing little treasure to gift yourself within the midst of a busy period. These little respites do wonders for restoring the nervous system and getting your happiness vibe back in the higher realms. When we take the time to restore, we are so much more powerful and productive in career and family experience.

4. Retreats. Whether you are going to a yoga or meditation retreat, or to a boot camp for speakers or authors, you will experience a total immersion into a new way of being. Hopefully, you will have chosen wisely and will get all the

boosting and energizing you require in order to take your next steps.

Brilliant ideas make you an extraordinary human being! If you don't already have a vacation on your schedule, now would be a good time to plan one.

Rejuvenating Rest

We have covered the kind of rest that comes from going on a great vacation. Now let's go over some basics so that you can experience restorative, restful time each day.

- Go to bed by 10 pm, and get 7–8 hours of sleep.
- Take a catnap when needed.
- Get a massage bi-monthly.
- Use a steam bath/sauna.
- Spend time relaxing by reading a good book.
- Go to a funny movie with friends and enjoy laughing.
- Have a sleep-in pajama day every once in a while. Take the phone off the hook and remember to breathe!
- Eat well, love well, play well, and rest. Life can be spectacular if you take the steps necessary to support your outrageous, great health!

CLEARING ENTANGLEMENTS FROM THE PAST

"LOVE, Love Love ... Love, Love Love ... Love, Love Love ...
There's nothing you can do that can't be done.
There's nothing you can sing that can't be sung.
There's nothing you can say, but you can learn
how to play the game ...
It's easy, so easy ...
All ya need is love. Do-do –do-do-oue ...
All ya need is love, love ... Love is all ya need."
—The Beatles

I wish you could have been with me the first time I held my daughter, Britta, in my arms. If you are a parent you know the feeling I am talking about. The sensation is like no other. If you were ever confused about what love is, you will find yourself to be totally, completely enraptured, and in love with this precious miracle—and the meaning of love takes on a whole new clarity.

I remember holding Britta's little, wet, naked body in my arms. "She's a girl"…with all her fingers and toes, a wisp of blonde locks matted down on her pointy, little cone head. Oh my god! I was overflowing with love and gratitude. I swear I felt like I would burst from the love, joy, and gratitude that consumed me at that moment.

That is the perfect love story. Just like that sweet romantic comedy you love so much—you know, the one where everything turns out so wonderfully in the end? This peak moment makes all the other less than heavenly moments dim in the shadow of the love and bonds that form in these precious seconds. It is a perfect time, and it is stellar.

Looking back on my daughter's birth, the part that I usually leave out is the other "stuff" concerning love. Just seconds after the doctor laid Britta on my tummy; my body was in crisis. I was slipping away though a medical condition that had been hidden until the moment of delivery. The placenta had torn away from the uterine wall perhaps two days prior. I had been hemorrhaging internally, and no one knew it until the "cork" came out. I could hear the nurses say they thought they were losing me. My young husband told them to be quiet in less than polite terms. Trays went flying. Icy cold, sterile instruments, and many hands entered my body to stop the bleeding.

Of course, the story has a happy ending. After a slow recovery of rebuilding my blood and strength, my love affair with Daughter Number One was firmly and completely established.

Love is everything. It is the few peak moments of stellar ecstasy, as well as the moments of trial and chaos. Love encompasses all realms of activity, emotions, and history. It is broad and deep and intense and messy, and it is what we are all here on this wonderful blue planet to learn and experience.

In the coming pages, you will examine your personal love space. We will completely focus on removing the limits and barriers that get in the way of you being the juicy, loving expression of yourself that you know you can be. I am so excited to share some fabulous methods with you for freeing up your love space so that you can be more fully present to all of your Bliss!

By Freeing Your Love Space, you will learn how to:

1. Clear pre-birth to present time contracts, entanglements, and agreements with your mother and father.
2. Magnetize your energy back to you and clear other people's residue out of your body.
3. Retrieve your energy and clean out unfilled dreams, disappointments, and old agreements with former spouses/lovers.
4. Clear DNA and family patterns related to your free and fun expression of love. This is an organized and systematic spiritual clearing that always works, and the results are phenomenal!
5. Remove impediments from your past lives (karma) in this present life.

The highest vibration in human relationships is the free flowing expression of love. It's what we live for and what we long for. What we're up to here involves your personal transformation in the primary domain, the realm of love. Bliss—your bliss here and now—is an inside job!

EXPELLING OBSTACLES ON THE PATH TO LOVE

In 1989, I went on a spiritual pilgrimage through India, traveling with a spiritual teacher, Guruji Keshavadas. The richness of the culture, the spirituality, and the natural way life integrated all aspects of daily routines so directly and quickly.

I had started following an Indian meditation path in 1984 when I met a practicing yogi while waitressing who taught me my first mantras. India, though, was when I began to learn the stories, and discover the real power and wonder of repetitive prayer and mantra.

Whenever a Hindu Indian starts any venture, they begin by asking the blessings of Lord Ganesha. He is the energy that dispels all obstacles from the path.

While I was touring in India with Guruji, we would go from temple to temple. He was quite the storyteller. Unlike the Christian model of purity and martyrdom, Hinduism was full of many divine beings. They had human qualities and lived as humans. They made human choices and were very much like us.

We would begin with a prayer to Lord Ganesha, who is a guide, just like Christians have angels and saints. Lord Ganesha's particular energy signature is that of clearing away what is in the way.

He, like many of us, had an interesting start…

From Indian Mythology, Lord Ganesha was born to THEE Goddess. Parvati, the equal and counterpart to Lord Shiva, held the power of creation and destruction.

As the story goes, Parvati was hanging out with her girls at the pools of her palace apartments. During a bout of unforgettable giggling and comparing notes in the baths, Parvati and her friends decided that it would be a great idea for the Goddess to create a son.

Parvati was left alone for extended periods of time while Lord Shiva was off doing "Important God Stuff," like meditating on Mount Kaylasi. Parvati wanted to create a son who would be obedient and devoted to her, and who would replace the long absent Lord Shiva. She used her Goddess power to control the three Gunas which are aspects of creation and the power of Genesis. She created a beautiful child. Her son was perfect, spotless, handsome and strong.

As time passed, he grew into a young man, and his mother trained him to be entirely available to serve her needs. He was cool with this because he didn't know he had a choice.

One day, his mother admonished him to protect her door with his life while she bathed. She said that it would make her feel very safe. He loved his mother, and his life was dedicated to serving her, so he became her bodyguard that day.

However, that very day, Lord Shiva returned from an extended meditation on the mountain. As he returned to his palace, all he could think about was finding his queen and feeling her tender, sweet body against his. As he approached her suite, walking briskly, he moved to the door where Ganesha was guarding his mother.

Lord Shiva demanded Ganesha move out of the way. Ganesha did not know this man was his father. A battle ensued. Shiva tricked Ganesha, and with one mighty swoop, he chopped the young man's head off with his dagger.

Parvati came running to the door and saw her beautiful son decapitated. She raged with a mother's fury and screamed at Lord Shiva to bring their son back, or she would never speak to him again. A surprised Shiva sprang into action. The head of his son had rolled off and could not be found, so he took his dagger and cut off the head of a passing regal elephant, restoring his son to his body with a new head.

There are five very useful elements from this story that we can use to explore your recovery of energy and self from your parental dynamics.

1. Pre-birth contracts
2. Chords
3. Family agreements, enculturation
4. Intense emotional timeline events
5. Enmeshments, entanglements

Pre-Birth Contracts

Lord Ganesha was created out of Parvati's desire for companionship, protection, and her emotional needs that were going unmet by her husband.

Write in your journal about three pre-birth contracts that might exist between you and your mother or father.

Chords

Chords automatically exist at birth between mother and child. Additional chords are created between people who share love, or who have a need to control. After age 16 or 18, we have no real need to be chorded to our parents.

Family Agreements, Enculturation

Family agreements and enculturation can be described as the way we are socialized. For example, my mother had emotional and mental troubles when I was little. My father expected me to help care for my mother and my brothers and sisters. My mother also looked to me to hold the family together. As the oldest daughter, I had a role as the subservient caretaker to my mother and the family.

Take a couple of minutes to reflect upon and journal about the possible family agreements that may, on some level, still affect you.

Intense Emotional Timeline Events

Having had his head chopped off by his father would impact Ganesha for the rest of his life unless the meaning or effect of the negative imprint was removed. As it turns out, Ganesha dispels obstacles, but his disfiguration left him without a love partner. He is one of the few Hindu Gods who is not a lover.

List several timeline events from your life that permanently changed you, in which you were living from "someone else's head."

Enmeshments, Entanglements

Enmeshments and entanglements show up when we get twisted up with others and don't have a clue as to why. Think back to a time when you felt like you were turning inside out after an interaction. Does that experience remind you of any event or programming from your childhood?

Believe in your capacity to heal.

Here are some Powerful Mantras I recommend:

Ganesha Mantra:

Vakratunda Maha Kaya
Koti Surya Samaprabha
Nirvighnam Kurumae Deva
Sarva Kayeshu Sarvada

Meaning: Remove the impediments from all the works we do, oh Lord Ganesha. You who shine the light of a million suns.

Use: Chant this mantra 10 times

~ ~ ~

Om Gum Rena Mochena
Ganapatiye Namaha

Meaning: Lord Ganesha, kindly remove all of my debts

Use: 108 times daily

~ ~ ~

Om Gum Kasepra
Ganapatiya Namaha

Meaning: Beloved Lord Ganesha, immediately assist me with an increased power of manifestation.

Use: 108 times daily.

COMPLETING WITH YOUR PARENTS—FORGIVENESS

To open your awareness, emotionally awaken, and experience your freedom to love, let's start at the beginning with yo' MAMA and yo' PAPA.

Were you blessed with perfect, loving, respectful, really cool parents? Remarkably, very few people are especially thrilled with the job their parents did for them when they were children.

When you think of your mother, what 3 or 4 words come to mind? When you think of your father, what 3 or 4 words come to mind?

The best way to complete with parents is to forgive them, to recognize they gave you everything they could, and let them off the hook for any ways you think they might have fallen short.

Forgiveness is the first step in creating completion, and for some, that will be a big stretch. Others may have already come to that. When we clear the timeline, you no longer need to hold onto the identity you have created out of the way your parents did, or didn't, give you what you needed.

It often surprises people to know that the challenges you created for yourself in this life were meant for you to learn and grow. In fact, you are the producer of your life and the casting director, who orchestrated a group of power players to give you great material from which you would learn and grow.

Write a letter of appreciation in your journal to the parents you cast in the roles you gave them. Thank them for what you have learned by having them in their primary role as your parents. Take 10 minutes for this exercise.

Candle Lighting and Completion

Symbolically, light a candle for each of your parents, holding them in light and appreciation. As the candles burn down, you will be in meditation, completing your karma with them.

In meditation, take the knowledge you have gleaned from your parents, and hand over any extraneous information (for example, what happened when an authority figure was cruel or inappropriate), to your Akashic record keeper, who will place all this knowledge in safe-keeping for you.

You can also practice the Lotus Mudra in front of your heart. Breathe up from heart three times and feel the energy go over your head each time. This practice will help to integrate the wisdom of your heart and the knowledge of your emotional body with the spiritual realm.

Love Yourself Now

It's time to be happy with who you are now. If all of your stories of past hardship toppled, and you were just you without any embellishments, would you like yourself? Are you living your life? Are you doing what you want to do?

LOVE GONE SOUTH—BREAKUPS AND DIVORCE

You are a work in progress! Yahoo! The person you were five years ago, or twenty years ago is not who you are now. People change and grow, and sometimes they outgrow each other.

One of the most amazing things to witness is how a couple reacts when there neither blames the other or has a need to make the other conform to the constructs of their own growth process. Having the spaciousness within to allow others to believe and think and experience the world from their own perspective is the most incredible gift you can give yourself and another. Instead of trying to control the world you live in so it fits with your view, you will get to see a multifaceted world of love, respect and diversity.

The opposite of this beautiful image I have just painted is that of the battle-oriented, wrong-making, opposite-sided fiasco where many couples wind up.

In Indian mythology, there is an amazing love story about Rama and Sita. All Hindus know and love these two characters, as well as Lord Hanuman.

The epic saga is called the Ramayana, and it tells the story of two lovers who were always meant to be together, but who were separated by others over and over again. At one point, Rama's stepmother tricks him into agreeing to live a life in the forest as an aesthetic. At another point, Sita is kidnapped by the demon, Ravana, and held prisoner in his woodland hideout. After 14 or so years of pining for, and longing for, each other, the lovers, who are husband and wife, finally settle into domestic bliss.

The couple experiences a few blissful weeks of making love and laughing with each other before Rama's captain's accuse Sita of having made love, or gone off willingly, with the demon. Sita pleads with her husband: "You are joking. Please… all these years, I have only thought of you, longed for you, kept you as my king."

But Rama's men continue to insist that the king must put her out or destroy her. A funeral pyre is lit and it looks like she will soon be burnt toast. But then Sita says, "I swear by the goddess I am not lying. I am pure and faithful to my husband. If I am lying, let the fires consume me."

She walks into the fire and emerges minutes later unharmed. Rama's mind is troubled. He cannot take her back, but he still loves her. So, he shuns her, and she is ostracized to an ashram a long distance from the kingdom.

Sita goes willingly, hoping he will have a change of heart. But Rama never calls for her again. Meanwhile, at the ashram, she discovers she is pregnant with twin boys. Her boys are beautiful and are raised as holy men, who recite scripture and sing praises to God. Their mother and father never work things out.

Rama is an example of a difficult divorce. Sita, having to prove her fidelity, is launched into the fire to prove her innocence, and still, she is rejected.

Embedded emotions, pain, and grief get stuck in the body. Through meditation, you can clear and release those energies that no longer support you.

Bummer Behaviors for Bad Break-Ups

Let us now look at the 3 common enmeshment and entanglement behaviors that often occur in bad break-ups.
1. Controlling/manipulating
2. Battling/anger and mudslinging
3. A gossiping/storytelling/trashing campaign

Controlling/Manipulating

Controlling or manipulating behaviors are stimulated by one's sense of insecurity and the misbelief that you will be okay as long as you keep the status quo. This kind of behavior erodes both your emotional body and that of your partner's. Truth and the ability to trust becomes a rare commodity when relationships degrade to this place, often resulting in the occurrence of energetic black splotches in the heart and lungs. The heart is the 5th brain; it is the love center. The lungs, when constricted, means that a person feels they do not have the right to take up space.

Battling, Anger, and Mudslinging

Battling, anger, and mudslinging is the direct approach to going for the jugular. With these behaviors, the fight is on. Sometimes people feel a need to be right and have the other be wrong. I do know that when things fall apart, it takes two to tango—both participants have a role in the demise of their relationship.

Battling—taking opposing sides—leaves little room for wise elder wisdom. The wise elder stance means that everyone has the right to a lifestyle, and life, they wish to create. No one, therefore, is wrong in their individual experience. However, the couple may no longer be a suitable match for co-habitation.

It's possible that 80–90% of the relationship was pretty good. But some deal-breakers surfaced. And once these deal-breakers came into the light, things necessarily needed to shift.

For example, a deal-breaker for Rama was losing the respect of his men. The deal-breaker for Sita was that she had lost the love and respect of her husband.

Gossiping/Storytelling/Trashing Campaign

A gossiping, storytelling, trashing campaign is a process that continually brings up an element of "what she or he did wrong." It is a bit like Post Traumatic Stress Syndrome. By constantly bringing the other's faults up, you keep validating the fact that this person and their wrongdoings hold great importance for you and that you are never going to forget it.

Negative Results from a Smear Campaign:

1. You cause a trauma to your own system that starts your emotional body believing that you are unlovable, because this person's actions would not be done to anyone they cherish or love. So, rather than the challenge of the experience as being a one-time event, you end up living with an ongoing, enormous invalidation that will keep on attracting more of the same.

    A good direction to go is to understand that your former partner is no longer a match for you. They have a right to be and express themselves in whatever ways they wish—but they can do those actions away from you.

2. You get other people enrolled in your smear campaign and they start to really hate your former lover. Guess what? You

can move into forgiveness, but it is highly unlikely that the friends you enrolled in being angry with your ex will ever change their attitude. Your internal experience is once-removed from them. Without real motivation to shift, they will continue to hold that belief in their emotional bodies. So, your former lover will indefinitely receive negative energy from all the folks who you enroll in a smear campaign.

On the other hand, your integrity and the respect of your friends rises when you go through a challenging spot without fault-finding or blame. Stay focused on yourself and your healing, and bring in balance, and you will rise in the eyes and the affection of those who love and care for you. (This is not to be confused with long-suffering martyrdom.)

If you recognize yourself engaging in any of the bummer behaviors above, can you upgrade your feelings and begin new conversations regarding the person you are no longer sharing love with?

Family, Friends and Foes

This last segment is dedicated to clearing relationships that have never been easy for you. Think of a family member or friend who you never got along with. This would be a person who you believe doesn't have a clue as to who you really are. Or perhaps the two of you came together very intensely and then a bomb went off between you, and your head is still spinning as you continue to wonder what happened.

The relationship I am describing here is a karmic relationship. Karmic relationships can feel old, complicated, and entangled even before they begin. This is the person you have known in your past lives.

Here are a few test statements to identify who this person might be in your life:

1. You feel twisted up inside when you think of them
2. You want out once and for all
3. You have cut them off or amputated them from your life
4. They have stopped speaking to you and have moved away

Take a moment to write the name of the person in your journal and write a statement or two about the nature of the dynamic you now have. What other descriptions or qualities describe the nature of this relationship for you?

Her is a strong example of a karmic relationship: Sa Jahan, the Ruler, and King of Agra had many wives and children. He was the 16th-century sovereign who built the great monument of love, the Taj Mahal, for his favorite wife and soul mate, Maharani.

From his oldest born boys, brothers all born to different mothers, came a horrific tale in their line of succession. This terrible story came about because Sa Jahan was completing his vision, which was to build a black Taj Mahal just across the river from the white one he had completed for his beloved. The foundation laid, he had spent much of his time and money on importing the most talented artisans and craftsmen from Portugal, Italy and India. The white Taj Mahal was created as a monument of love for Ma hisharani, and was the fulfillment of a promise to her; she had perished after a difficult childbirth, and this had broken his heart. He swore to her he would build a monument reflecting their love and there she would rest.

Once completed, he had the foundation built for the reflective tomb in which his body would rest upon his passing.

Son Number 3 became greedy, seeing his father pouring all the funds of the kingdom into this monument. So, he created a diabolical plot to overthrow the king.

This meant he would kill his first and second born brothers, which he did, and then defeat the king and imprison him for the remaining years of his life. Sa Jahan lived out his days in a red fort, a prisoner of his 3rd son. He never completed his parallel resting place, and his tomb is stuck oddly next to the perfectly placed grave of his beloved wife.

The family complications here are great examples of karmic relationships: the 3rd son, being jealous of the first two brothers' positions, literally kills them off, then overthrows the king, but doesn't kill him. Rather, he imprisons him.

Think about your story. Do you have an epic Taj story yourself? A story you thought should have been a great love story, but it ended up being a story where the relationship was severed, or left you feeling imprisoned?

Think of this person, who plays a challenging role in your life. Maybe you killed them off in your way or imprisoned them, or vice versa.

Releasing and letting go of the past, taking responsibility and making amends is the path to health and happiness.

CONCLUSION

As you have read these pages you have gotten a chance to look more deeply into your life patterns. What you choose and how you allow life to play out. I've invited you to step into the next best expression of self and become the person you know you can be.

You are special, my friend. Know that you are loved and wanted. Your life matters and just by being you, nothing more, you make the world a better place.

I believe in you and your capacity to heal.

All my love,
Julie Renee

THINGS OUR ATTORNEY WANTS US TO SHARE WITH YOU

The content case studies and examples in this book do not in any way represent the "average" or "typical" member experience. In fact, with any program offering a way to improve health, vitality, wealth and love, we know that some members purchase our systems and never use them, and therefore, get no results from their membership at all. You should assume that you will obtain no results from this program. Therefore, the member case studies we are sharing can neither represent nor guarantee the experience of past, current or future program participants or members. Rather, these unique case studies represent what is possible with our system. Each of these unique case studies, and any and all results reported in these case studies by individual members, are the culmination of numerous variables, many of which we cannot control, including pre-existing mental, emotional, and health conditions; personal incentives; discontinuity of spiritual and energetic conditions; and countless other tangible and intangible factors.

Whether this notice refers to "you" or "your," it means you; the pronouns "we" or "our" refer to Gable-Kennedy Inc., dba "One Hundred Percent You."

Any improvements in health, mindset, and energy are examples of what we think you can achieve. However, we make no assurances; you'll do as well if you rely only on the assurances in this book, but you must also accept the risk of not doing as well.

Specific health activations have, for many, returned their health to high function. Examples of successful healings are used in this book and attributed to the individuals/participants who have experienced these shifts through the One Hundred Percent Healthy individual and group programs. There is no assurance you will do as well. If you rely on our reports of transformation, you must also assume the risk of not doing as well.

Any representation of improved health, wealth, relationship and mindset in this book, our websites, and our programs are not considered to be average or normal. Likewise, any claims or representations from our course participants and students are not considered to be average results.

There can be no assurance that any prior successes, or past results, regarding health, wealth, love, and relationship success can be used as an indication of future results.

Returning health, energy, clarity and ease to the body are based on many factors. We have no way of knowing how well you will do, as we do not know you, your background, your ability to heal, your work ethic or basic health and body care practices. Therefore, we do not guarantee or imply that you will have improvements or achieve better health, wealth, relationships, love, money, or any other improvements suggested in this book, on our website, or anywhere else. If you rely only on the assurances in this book you must accept the risk of not doing as well.

The "One Hundred Percent Healthy" and "One Hundred Percent You" programs are designed for people who are already healthy and want to take their health to the next level. Your health, wealth and love are entirely in your hands. Our programs are meant to be educational in nature, so these programs may not be suited for everyone. Making decisions based on any information presented in our products, services, or website should be done only with the knowledge that you could experience significant losses, make no improvement at all, or achieve no desired result regarding your health, wealth, relationships, and energy.

Use caution and seek the advice of qualified professionals. Check with your health care director, therapist, or professional business advisor, before acting on this or any other information found in this book.

Users of our products, services and website are advised to do their own due diligence when it comes to making health decisions and all information, products, and services that have been provided should be independently verified by your own qualified professionals. Our information, products, and services on www.julierenee.com should be carefully considered and evaluated, before reaching a business decision about whether to rely on them.

You agree that our companies are not responsible for the success or failure of your health, wealth, or relationship decisions relating to the information presented by www.julierenee.com or our companies' products or services.

PRECIOUS ADVICE
JUST FOR YOU FROM JULIE RENEE

Let me help you take your next step!

You've gotten a lot of great information in this book, and hopefully a lot of value, too. If you're like me, you'll want to learn how you can take this work to the next level and get your life skyrocketing with better health, energy, connection and momentum. Since no two people are exactly alike, I'd like to suggest five choices about ways to take your 100% pursuit into your life. Keep in mind I have been teaching and assisting folks with health for more than two decades and am prolific. I encourage you to explore the www.JulieRenee.com website and discover a wealth of mini-programs and directed meditations, if you would like to jump in with baby steps.

If, however, you like to take action in a big way and are ready to have it all, here are the three paths to choose from on JulieRenee.com:

1. 100% You Assessment and free programs for increasing energy and wealth

2. The Quantum Immersion program: Discover the full Divine Human Blueprint for personal and professional use. The program includes a twelve-month training.

3. VIP Mentoring Experience: Intimate one to one experience with Julie Renee. Receive personal hours of directed quantum energy activating shifts in perception, brain, energy, and all aspects of the human dynamic. This is followed up by three months of personalized mentoring and master's programs for full one hundred percent healthy, happy results.

Terms of Use – Disclaimer

The purpose of this book is to educate and entertain. The author and publisher do not guarantee that anyone following the techniques, suggestions, tips, ideas, or strategies will be successful. The author and publisher shall have neither liability nor responsibility to anyone with respect to any loss or damage caused, or alleged to be caused, directly or indirectly by the information in this book.

ABOUT THE AUTHOR

Julie Renee refuses to play small. She powerfully mentors those who are being taken out of the game with exhaustion and "fuzzy brain." She regenerates the brain and gets them back to playing at 100% again.

Books by Julie Renee are *100% You, Your Divine Human Blueprint,* and *Balance Your Life Now!*

Julie Renee is the founder and developer of a new spiritual science, the 100% Healthy Human Blueprint. She is the author of the ground-breaking book, Your *Divine Human Blueprint.* Her unique gift of healing defines the energy-science of Cellular Quantum Mechanics. She trains individuals in her "100% You Immersion Program" and sees private VIP clients in her home in northern California.

After launching her first business from her tiny San Francisco studio apartment in 1993, she has prevailed over a challenging history of multiple cancers and five near-death experiences. Overcoming tremendous odds, none of her doctors saw a possibility for her to survive her illnesses; she was repeatedly told she was dying.

Unwilling to believe that this was true, even the Angel of Death could not convince her that it was her time to go. She has dedicated her life to the betterment of humankind and the reawakening of humanity to the Divine Human Blueprint.

Recognized for her leadership abilities, she is the recipient of the 2010–2011 National Association of Professional Women's "Woman of the Year Award" and the Powerful Women International's "Global Leadership Award" 2012.

Julie Renee has been featured as an expert on CBS, Unity FM, Rock Star Radio, Blog Talk Align, Live 365, Low Down, *Spirit Seeker, 11: 11 Magazine, Spirit Seeker Magazine,* and on various TV shows, including "New Era Healing" and a "Forum on Spirituality." She is a writer for *Holistic Fashionista Magazine* and *Accomplish Magazine*. She is also the host of the radio show, *100% Healthy*. Additionally, she has both stage and film credits, and is a harpist and singer.

Julie Renee is *the* 100% Healthy Life EXPERT. She helps women succeed in life and business by activating them simply and easily to get to 100% in both health and vitality. An expert meditation instructor, she shares the secrets of altering reality through meditation, and provides an integrated fast track for manifesting, holding and growing abundance, health, beauty, and wealth. Her home activation programs include the following:

- Beautiful From the Inside Out
- Accelerate Wealth 21 - Day Program
- Illumination Rosary for Enlightenment
- The Sound of Truth - Vedic Mantra for transformation
- Your Secret Keys audio series
- The Definitive Guide to Meditation series
- Your Divine Human Blueprint home study audio series
- Unlimited Love

As a speaker, she has shared the stage with Marci Shimoff, Jack Canfield, Caterina Rando, James Malinchak, Sean Aston, Stedman Graham, Julie Carrier, Dr. Bill Dorfman, Jill Lublin, PJ Van Hulle, and many others.

From Farm Wife to Health Activator

Julie Renee started out in Minnesota as a farm wife, attended art school, modeled, waitressed, appeared in seven films, became a very successful realtor, and finally moved into her passion as a healer in the form of a health activator. She now has over thirty years' experience supporting individuals and groups in Quantum Health Activations, from high-risk pregnancies to life-saving interventions with critically ill individuals. Known as the premier healer for high risk pregnancies, twenty doctors and six midwives sent their most difficult clients to Julie Renee to help them from gestation through the first year after birth. In all, she has assisted more than one hundred and forty high risk babies to successfully enter this world.

Many years ago, she taught yoga and offered healing massage to people in recovery. She also taught infant massage, worked with insurance companies, and helped injured clients return to living, and hospice clients pass from this world, pain-free and without medication as they said good-by to their loved ones.

Moving deeper into her exploration of regeneration, she developed specialized Jadeite hot stone treatments, accessing the knowledge of the ancient civilizations of the Olmecs and Mayans, who used Jadeite for body initiations and transformations.

As part of a natural progression, Julie Renee moved from physical healing to offering spiritual life coaching for women. Through her clairvoyant gifts, she helped women rapidly shift to move into their next highest step.

For the past seven years, Julie Renee has been researching and developing programs with the Blueprint, teaching through guidebooks, courses and meditation as a simple way to access the healing gifts and secrets of the Divine Human Blueprint.

Thousands of individuals have created health, wealth and love with Julie Renee's help. Through her extraordinary gifts, she has brought critically ill people back into their lives, restoring health to their cellular and energetic bodies through the Divine Human Blueprint.

Traveling the world, she has studied in India, and is both an ordained minister and a pujari (carrier of the light) in the yogic tradition.

Julie Renee's favorite vacations include rappelling down waterfalls, zip lining, and performing daring acts, such as shooting down the longest water slide in Mexico. She loves the ocean, the mountains, and nature, and is a nature girl at heart. You can find her out hiking trails every chance she gets. She challenges herself regularly by rappelling, and doing other fun but scary activities that involve hanging from great heights with ropes. Her favorite ice cream is rose petal. She loves mangos and scented flowers, especially garden roses.

Julie Renee can be reached through her website at:
www.JulieRenee.com
or on any of the following social sites: Facebook, YouTube, LinkedIn, Twitter, and Pinterest

www.ingramcontent.com/pod-product-compliance
Lightning Source LLC
Chambersburg PA
CBHW061658040426
42446CB00010B/1800